# BURIED SAN FRANCISCO BAY AREA

## THE FALLEN STAR

JESSICA FERRI

AMERICA
THROUGH
TIME

America Through Time
Fonthill Media LLC
www.through-time.com

First published 2025

Copyright © Jessica Ferri 2025

ISBN 978-1-62545-159-0



Typeset in 10pt on 13pt Sabon
Printed and bound in England

All images were taken by the author unless otherwise noted.

# Contents

# About the Author

Jessica Ferri is a writer and photographer based in Northern California. She is the author of *Silent Cities New York* and *Silent Cities San Francisco*, and a book critic for the *Los Angeles Times* and the *Washington Post*. She is the owner of the feminist bookshop Womb House Books.

# INTRODUCTION

It's strange to write a book on San Francisco cemeteries, because there are very few cemeteries in San Francisco. There is the cemetery in the churchyard of Mission Dolores, the San Francisco Columbarium, and the National Cemetery in the Presidio. But those are few burial places for a living population of approximately 800,000 people. With the Golden Gate Bridge, the stunning views of the Bay Area, and its moody, foggy microclimates, San Francisco is one of America's most beautiful cities. The cemeteries are missing, but no one's too concerned about how they disappeared.

You can catch a glimpse of their remains all over the city. At Buena Vista Park, cracked pieces of tombstones line the gutters. On sidewalks, epitaphs pop up from tombstones that once belonged to four of San Francisco's epic Victorian cemeteries: Laurel Hill, Masonic, Odd Fellows, and Calvary. There were also two Jewish cemeteries near Mission Dolores Park, and a large City Cemetery where Lincoln Golf Course and the Legion of Honor now stand. At Ocean Beach, when the tide is right, large tombstones appear in the sand, thrown onto the beach, discarded. Many assume that the cemeteries of San Francisco were damaged in the 1906 earthquake and the broken stones incorporated into city projects. They aren't wrong; but that doesn't explain their disappearance from the city.

San Francisco's cemeteries were evicted by the city itself. By the early 1900s, thanks to the Gold Rush and a steady influx of immigrants both domestic and foreign, San Francisco was in desperate need of space. A decision was made in 1912 to bar new burials within city limits. But that wasn't enough, and development called for more. Cities are made for the living, after all. San Francisco was not the first city that had considered this: New York and plenty of others moved cemeteries in their early days or barred burials in existing cemeteries—but none have done so at the scale and the late timing of San Francisco's undertaking.

In 1914, the city decided the big four cemeteries would have to go. Colma, a city just south of Daly City, was chosen as the new resting place for San Francisco's dead. The relocation process was an arduous and complicated ordeal that took nearly twenty years. One can imagine the enormous, backbreaking labor of transferring hundreds of thousands of burials without the help of modern technology.

As time has passed, it's become very clear that the process was never completed. Graves from San Francisco's original cemeteries are frequently uncovered. In 1993, 750 graves were discovered in the renovation of the Legion of Honor museum. Upwards of 17,000 people are believed to still rest under the Legion of Honor and the adjacent Lincoln Golf Course. This was once City Cemetery, the resting place of immigrants, the Chinese, the homeless, and the civic dead. When the relocation efforts began, the city promised they would move loved ones with honor to Colma—but in mass graves. If families wanted to maintain their private plots and headstones, there was a fee. While those left behind may have been overlooked due to unavoidable human error, there was also a clear division between the rich and poor, even in death. Indigenous burial grounds were never considered for protection or relocation. White settlers simply bulldozed sacred shell mounds all over the Bay Area and developed right on top. As a result, there are countless apartment buildings and retail stores that rest on top of sacred burial sites.

My first book on San Francisco's cemeteries, *Silent Cities: San Francisco*, was published in October 2021. I spent all of 2020 and the first part of 2021 researching and writing the book during lockdown during the Covid-19 pandemic. My son, who was two at the time, wasn't able to attend preschool, because the schools were closed. We spent much of our time in Colma, where the dead outnumber the living 1,000 to 1. The cemeteries were quiet; they were incredibly beautiful. They were a welcome respite to us, desperate for a way to get outside safely. As a photographer and writer, I spend much of my time thinking about death and the ways in which people are treated in life and death. It was an odd feeling to be dealing with a mass death event while I wrote that book.

Because of the lockdown, not all the cemeteries I wanted to visit were open to the public. Mountain View, in Oakland, very kindly allowed me to tour the cemetery twice while they were closed. I'm accustomed to being mostly alone when I visit a cemetery, but those two trips were something I will never forget. The cemetery is fairly large, but if you're eager and mobile enough, it's walkable. It was downright eerie to know as I walked through Mountain View that there was not another single living soul on the grounds aside from the occasional landscaper zipping by on a golf cart.

Other cemeteries, like the Columbarium, weren't open to my visit during lockdown. As an active mortuary, that decision made sense. But the Columbarium doesn't appear in *Silent Cities: San Francisco*. I'm very happy to say that the Columbarium is part of this book. Not only is the Columbarium an active mortuary and cemetery, the people who work there are wonderful human beings, dedicated to serving their community.

It's understandable that most people would like to have death out of sight, and therefore, out of mind. At one time, perhaps, it was possible to forget that death is real in San Francisco. But I think—or rather, I hope—that since the years of the pandemic, this is not the case. An epidemic levels the playing field. Like an earthquake, everyone is stopped in their tracks. It's in that moment waiting for the worst that we are perhaps the most human—promising ourselves that we'll do better, that we'll live more gratefully— if the earth doesn't give way beneath us. Like the plight of the human race during the pandemic, some of us were more at risk than others. That moment that puts us all at risk—the inevitable realization of our own mortality—is what reminds us of what it means to be human. A little reminder of that now and then can never be a bad thing, especially if it comes in the form of a historic, beautiful communal space like a burial ground.

The cemeteries of San Francisco, in their absence from the city of their creation, have much to tell us—if we only stop for a moment and pay attention.

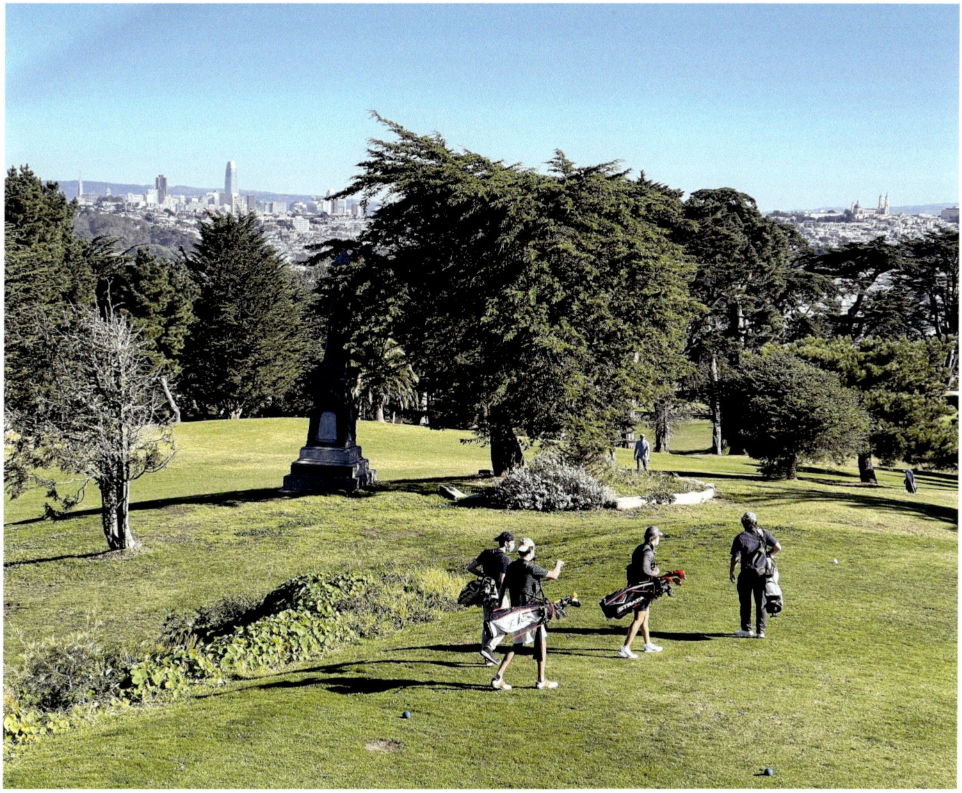

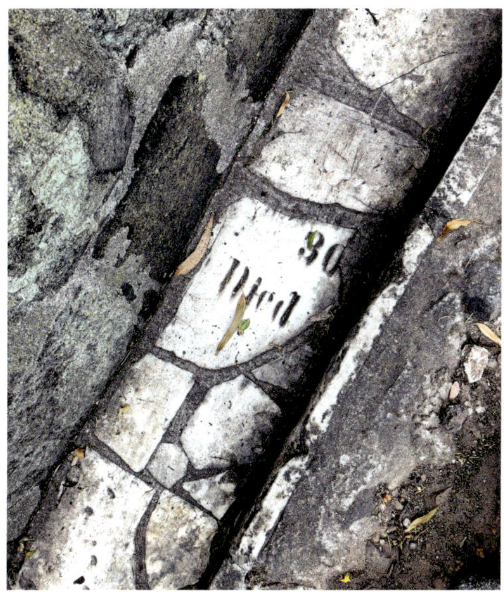

A round of golf at Lincoln Park, built on top of the remains of City Cemetery.

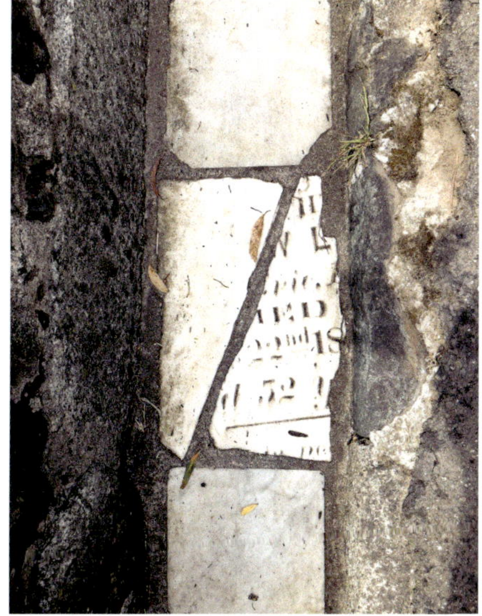

Tombstones used in the gutters at Buena Vista Park.

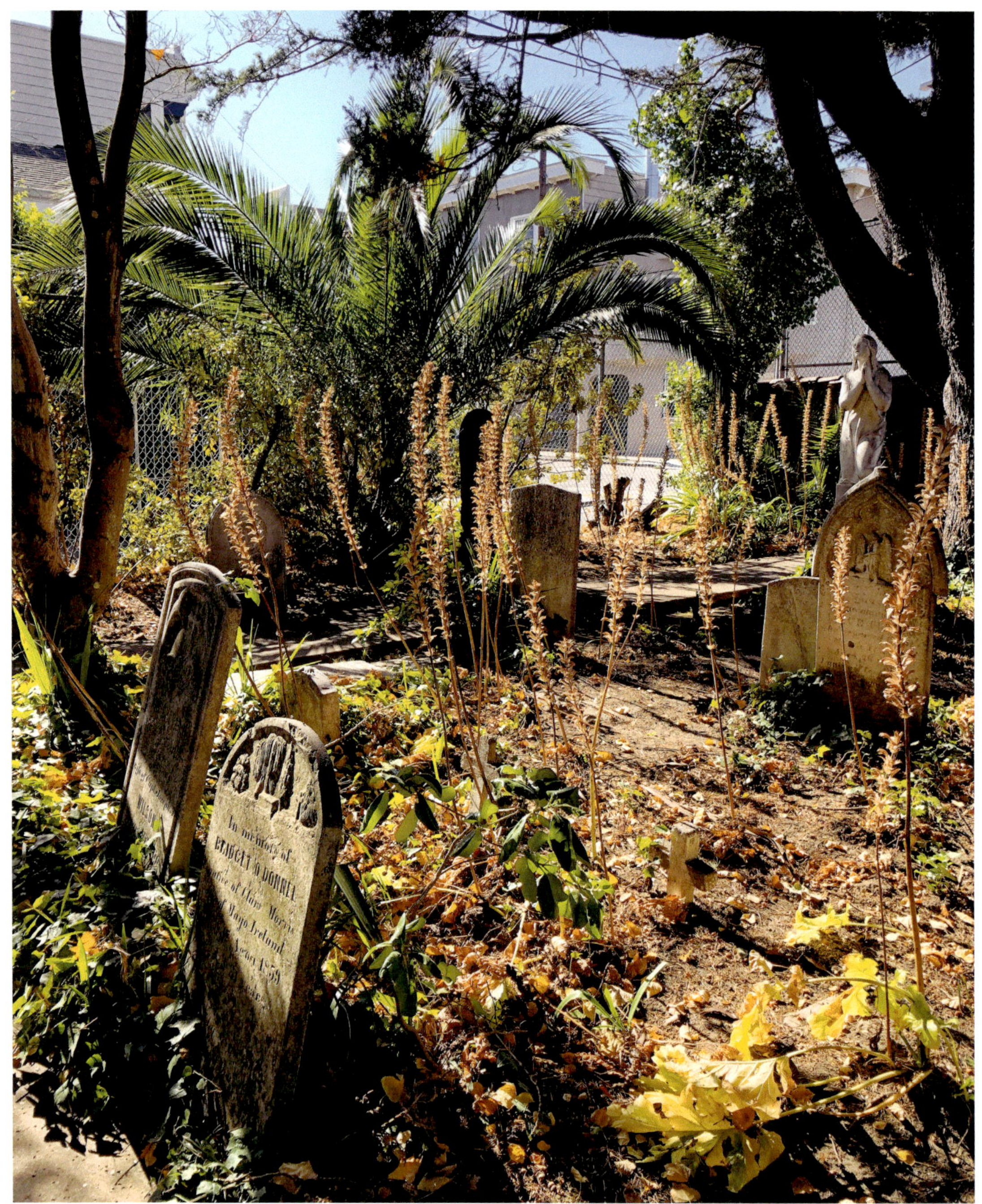

*Above and next page:* Mission Dolores cemetery, one of the only remaining cemeteries in San Francisco city limits.

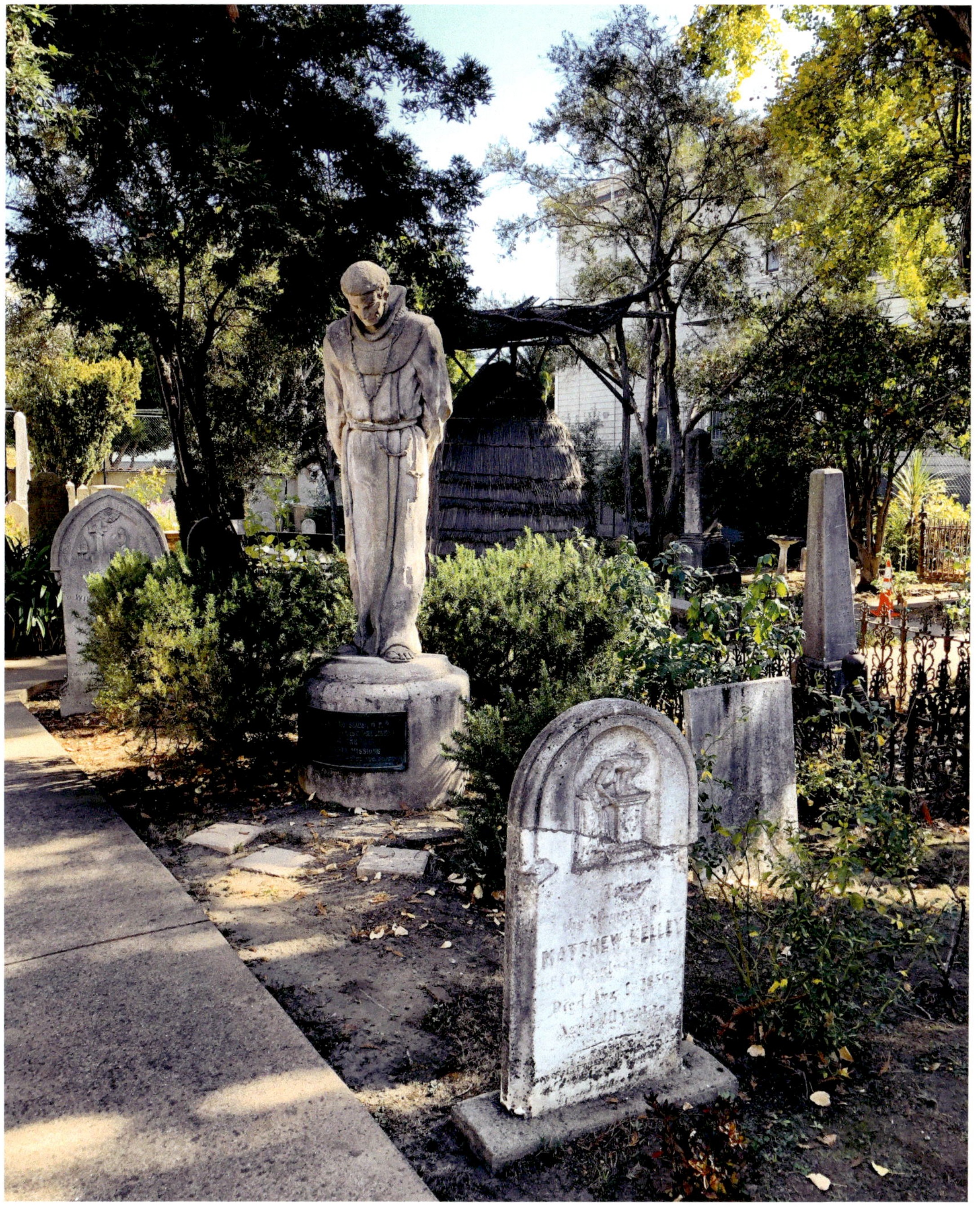

# 1
# THE SAN FRANCISCO COLUMBARIUM

A Columbarium is similar to a mausoleum; however, rather than crypts for caskets, a Columbarium houses niches for cremains, usually stored in urns. The San Francisco Columbarium was once a part of Odd Fellows Cemetery, which covered the surrounding 30 acres. When cemeteries were evicted from the city, and the moving process to Colma took place, the Odd Fellows' Columbarium remained in San Francisco.

Over the ensuing years, the Columbarium changed hands and fell into disrepair. Luckily, the Neptune Society bought this important part of San Francisco history and began restoration. Today, the Columbarium is an active mortuary and funeral home. And yes, there are still niches available.

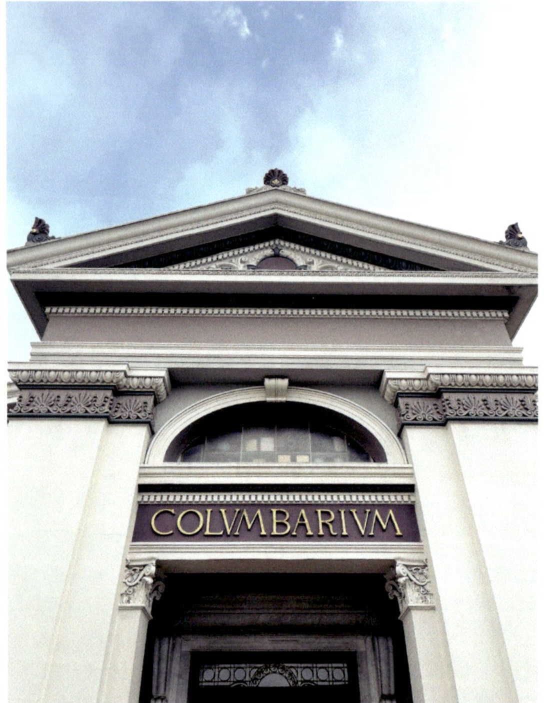

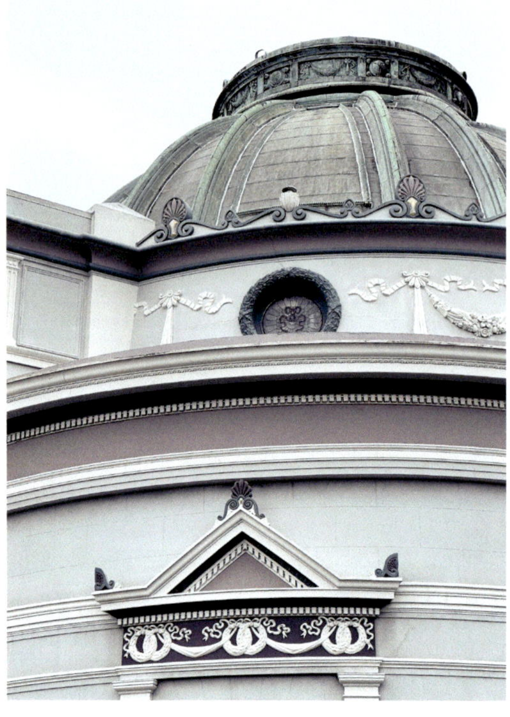

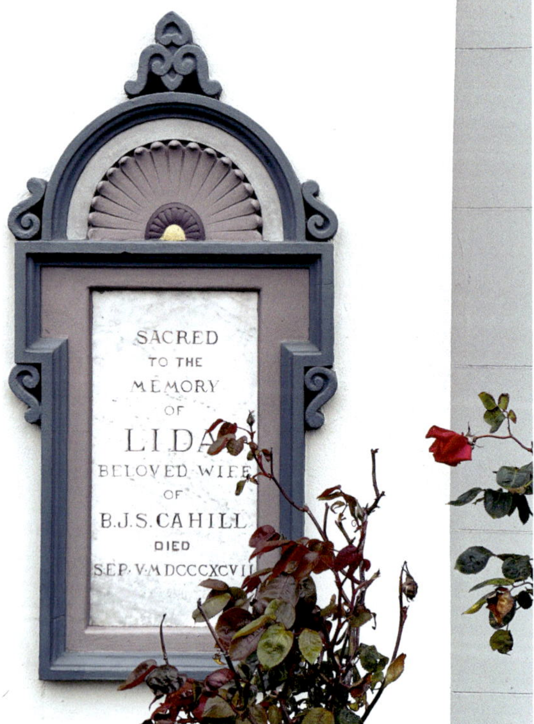

*These pages:* The entrance to the San Francisco Columbarium, once part of Odd Fellows Cemetery.

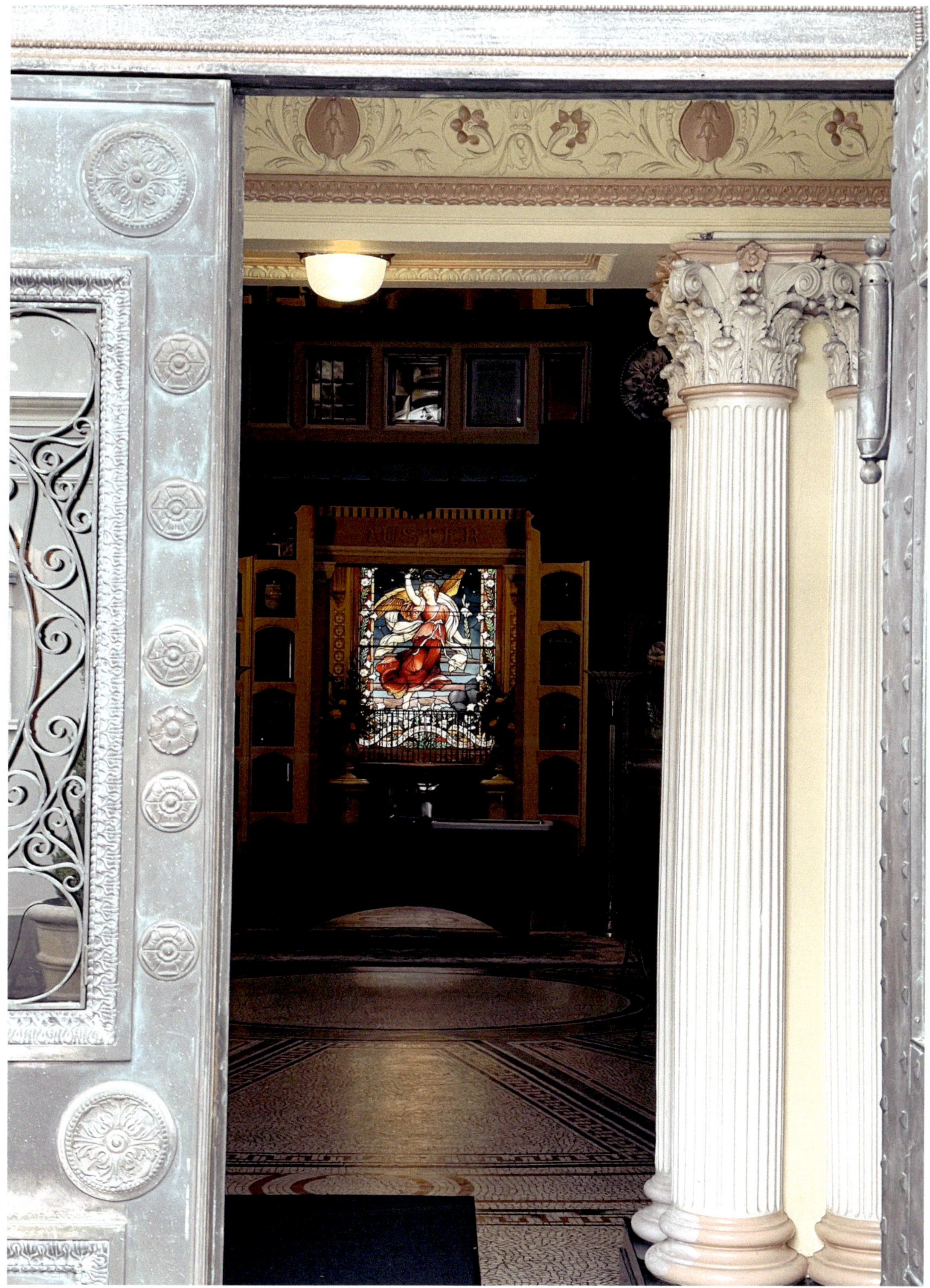

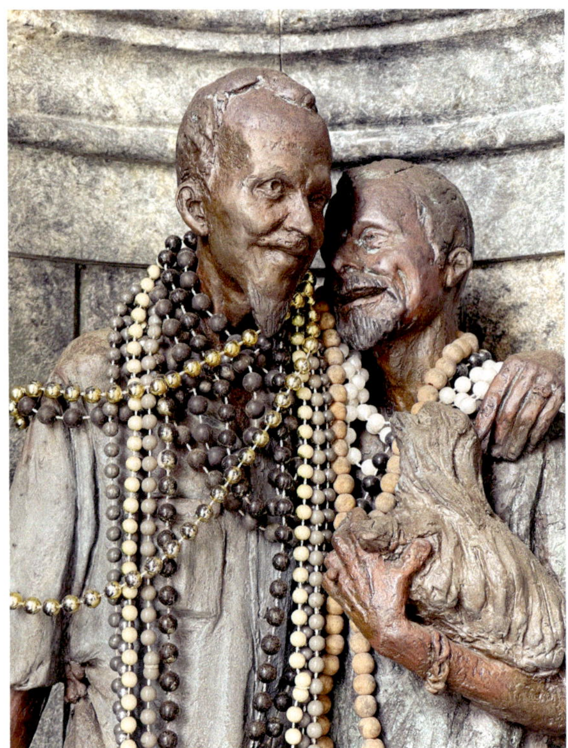

A couples' memorial near the entrance to the Columbarium. The funeral home at the Columbarium worked steadily in service to families during the AIDS epidemic and is a mainstay of support in the LGBTQ+ community.

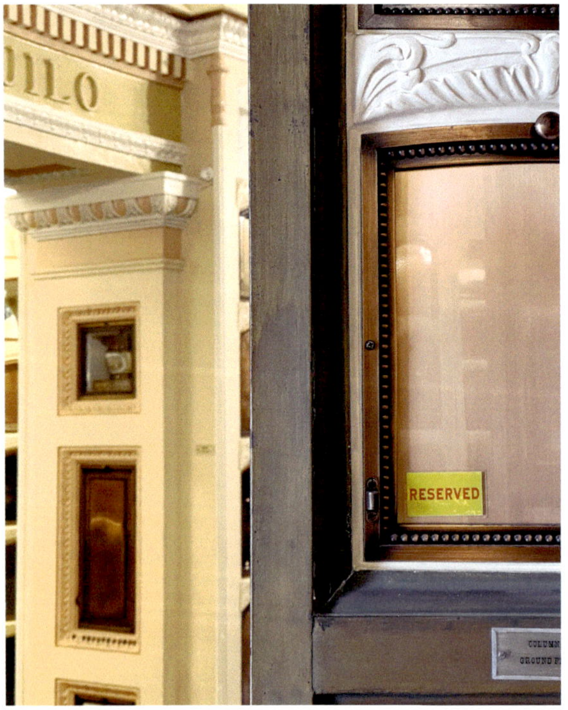



The Columbarium is an active funeral home, and there is still space inside this historic landmark.

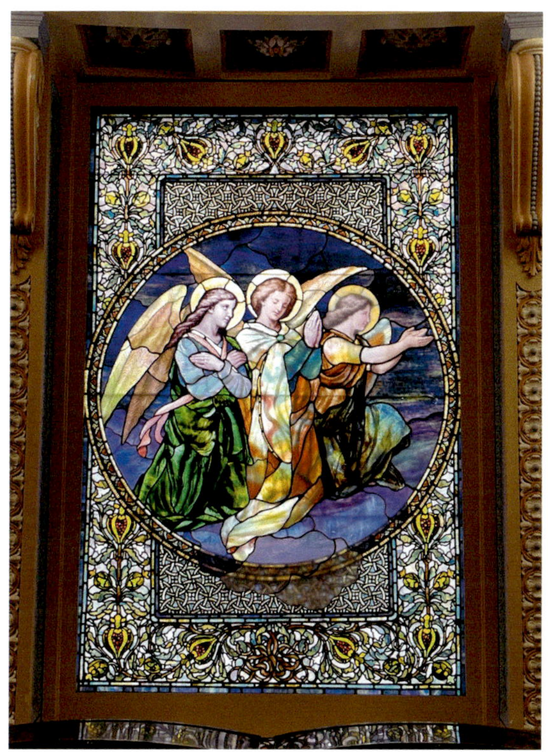

One stained-glass window inside,
attributed to Louis Comfort Tiffany.

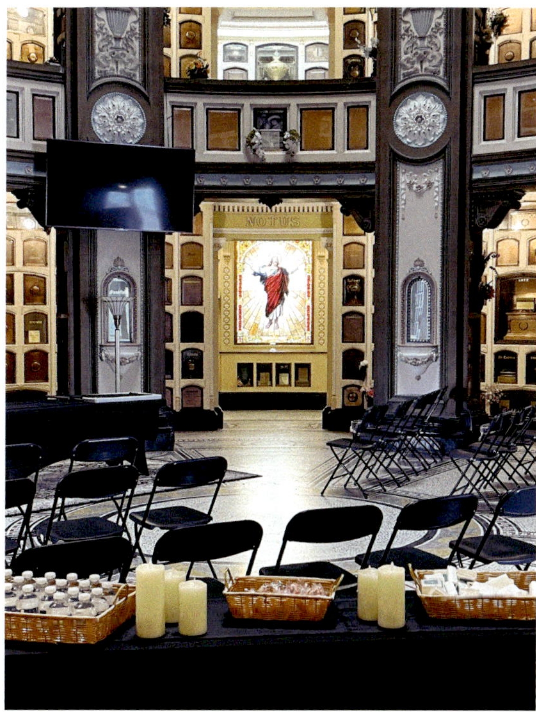

The Columbarium is committed to serving
the Bay Area community through events
and educational happenings.

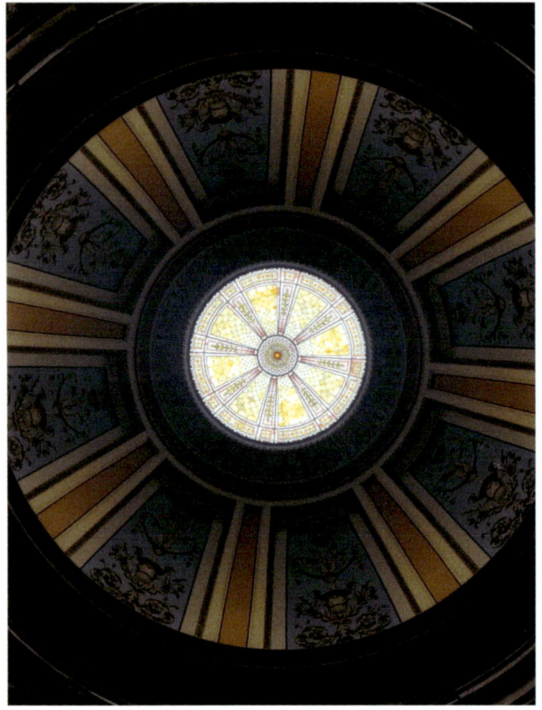

The Columbarium's domed ceiling also contains a stained-glass window.

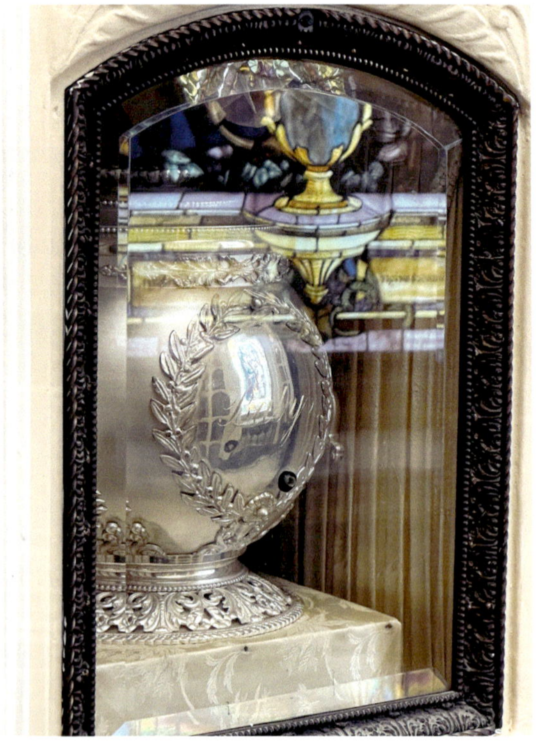

The urns inside the niches are astounding—many are made from sterling silver and bronze.

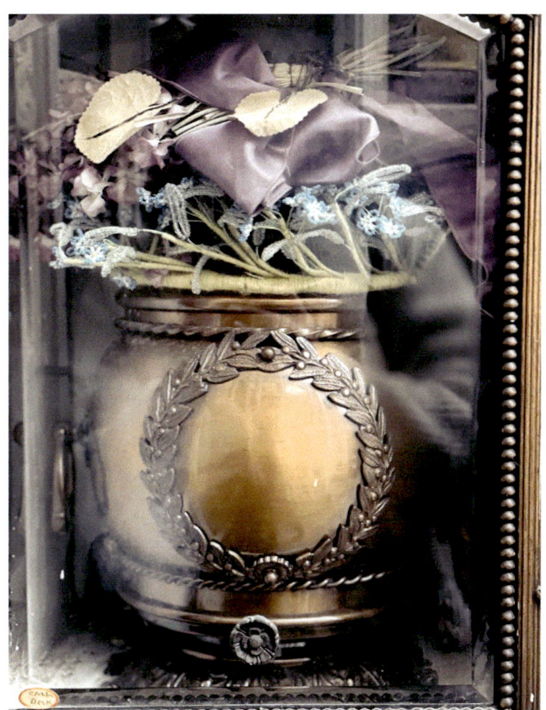

This one still features beautiful ribbons and dried flowers.

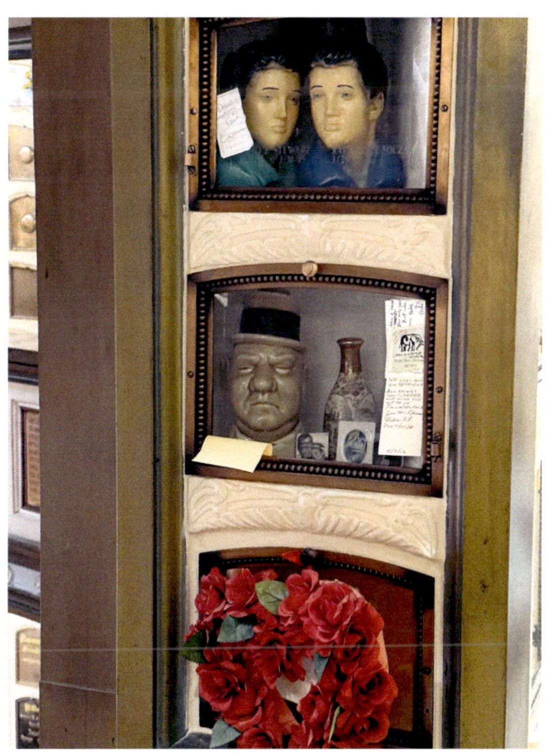

Some delightful design choices for urns.

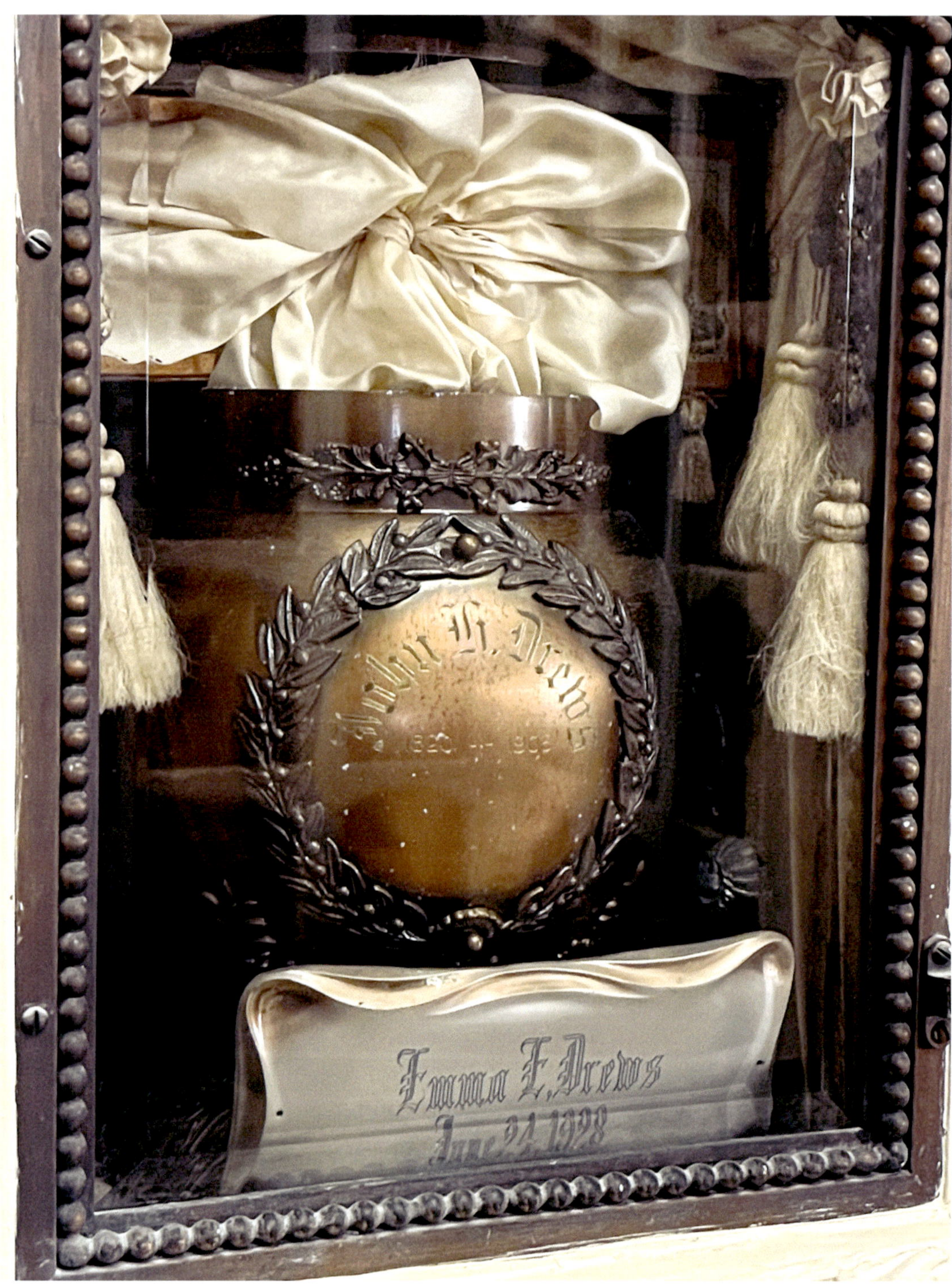

Gorgeous bows and tassels.

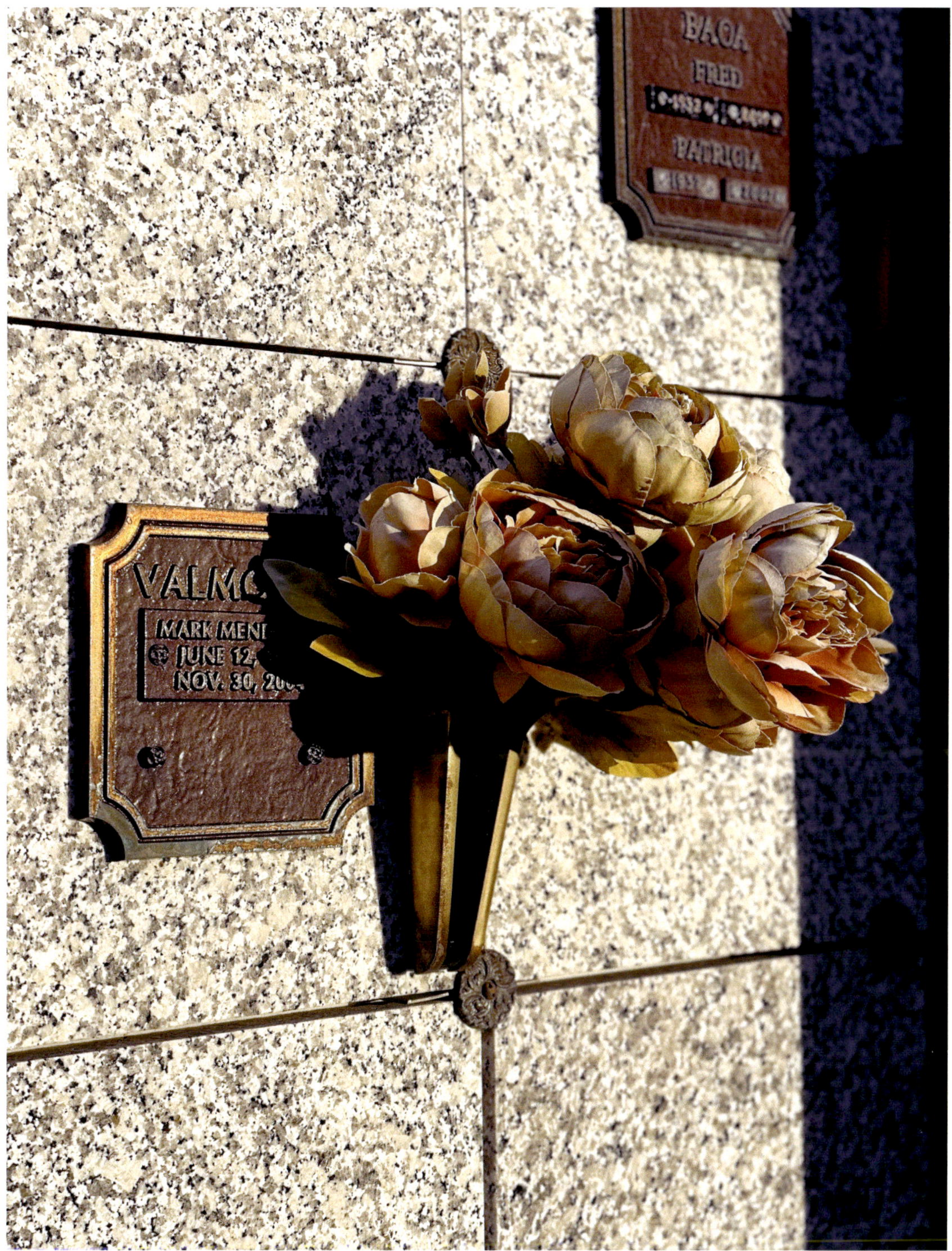

The Columbarium was renovated in the 1980s and expanded to include wall crypts and in-ground burials on its grounds.

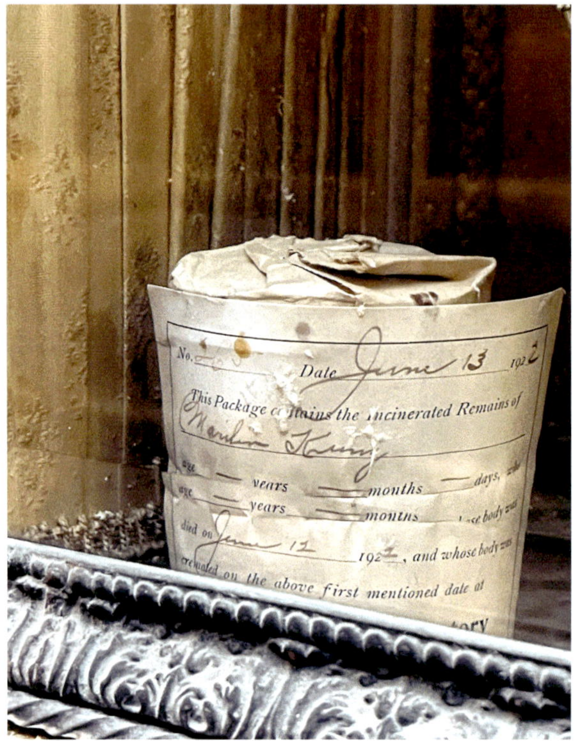



A less formal container for "incinerated remains."

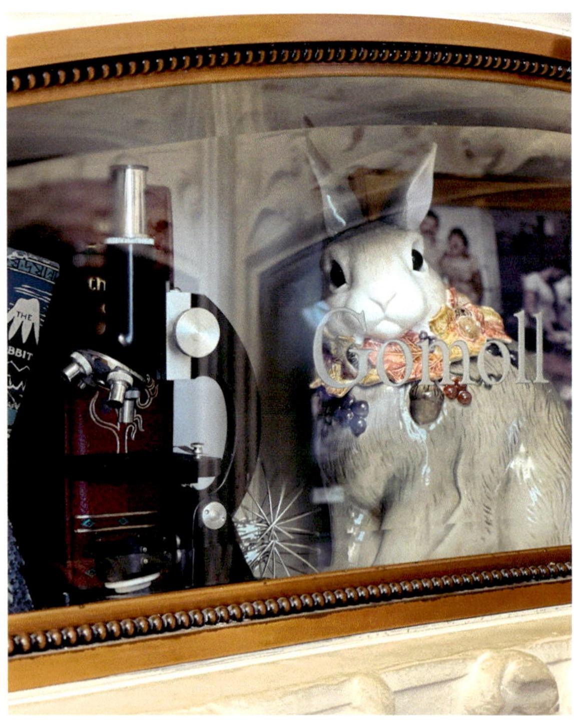



A bunny urn inside a niche with personal items relevant to the occupant's life.

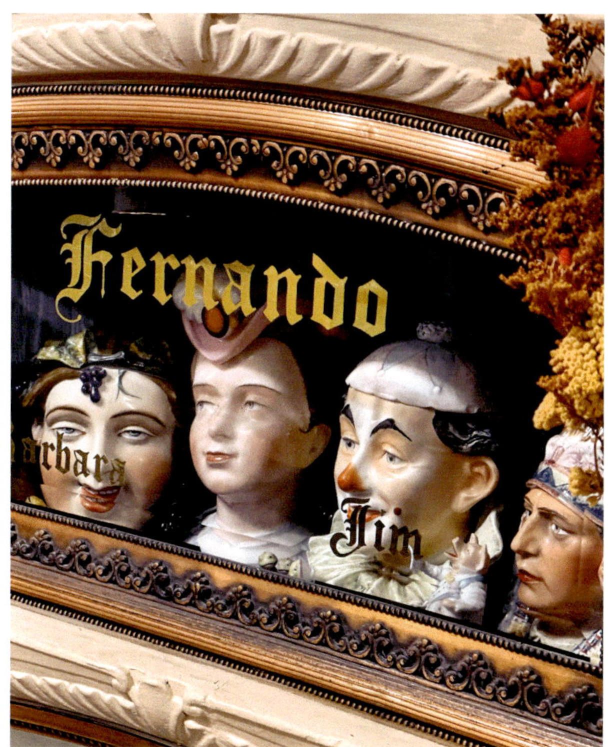



*Right:* Comedia dell'Arte character urns.

*Below left:* Some niches contain beautiful portraits of their occupants.

*Below right:* At the end, it's true.

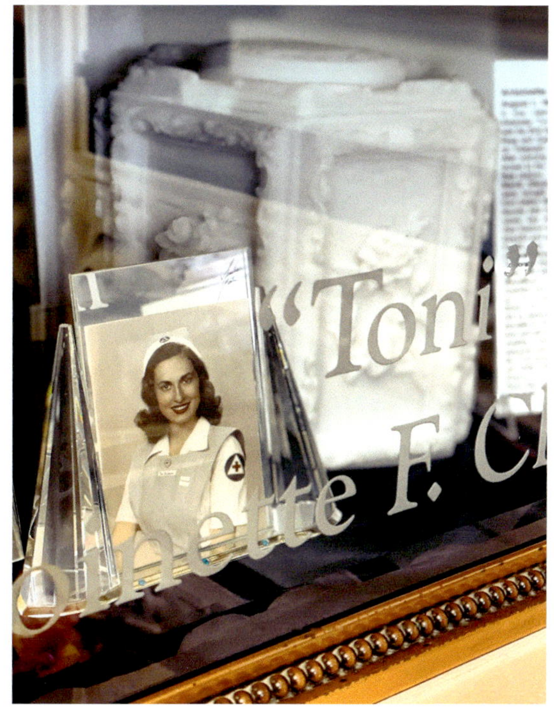

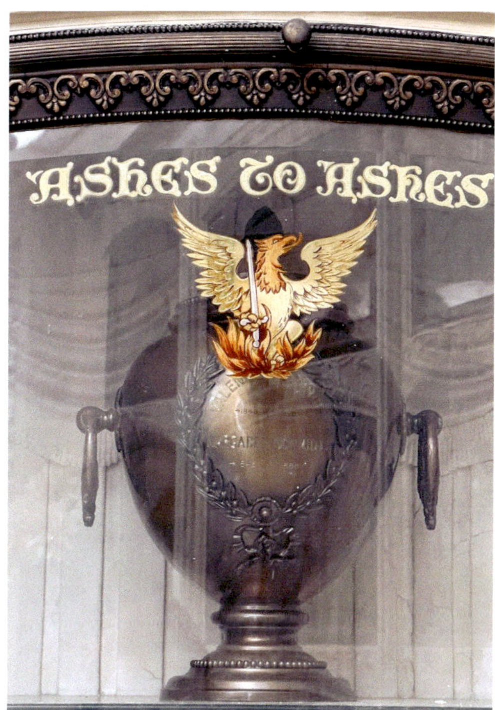

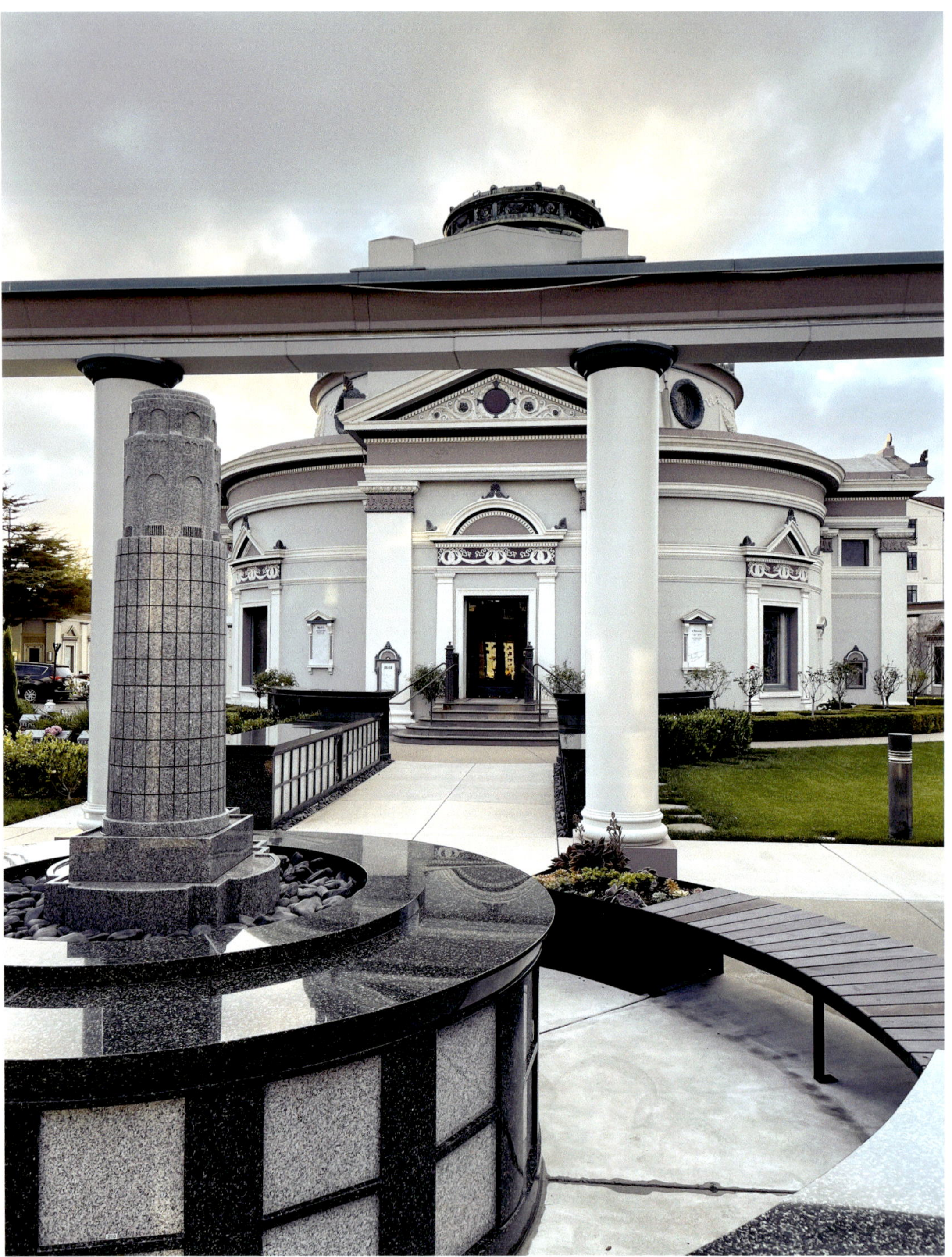

A sunset view of the Columbarium.

# 2
# MOUNTAIN VIEW CEMETERY, OAKLAND

The cemeteries of the East Bay were lucky to avoid the relocation movement, being outside city limits already. Mountain View Cemetery, now known as the Piedmont Cemetery, is a gorgeous example of a Victorian Park (or Rural) cemetery. It was designed by Frederick Law Olmstead, the designer of Manhattan's Central Park.

Mountain View was designed with the living in mind. Like Mount Auburn Cemetery, in Cambridge, Massachusetts, or Green-Wood Cemetery, in Brooklyn, New York, other rural cemeteries in the U.S., Mountain View was meant to be a place for the living to enjoy, with strolls, picnics, and other appreciations of life through nature and beauty.

Many of the most wealthy and prominent Bay Area families are buried here, mostly notably in a row of mausolea with a great view of the city nicknamed "Millionaire's Row."

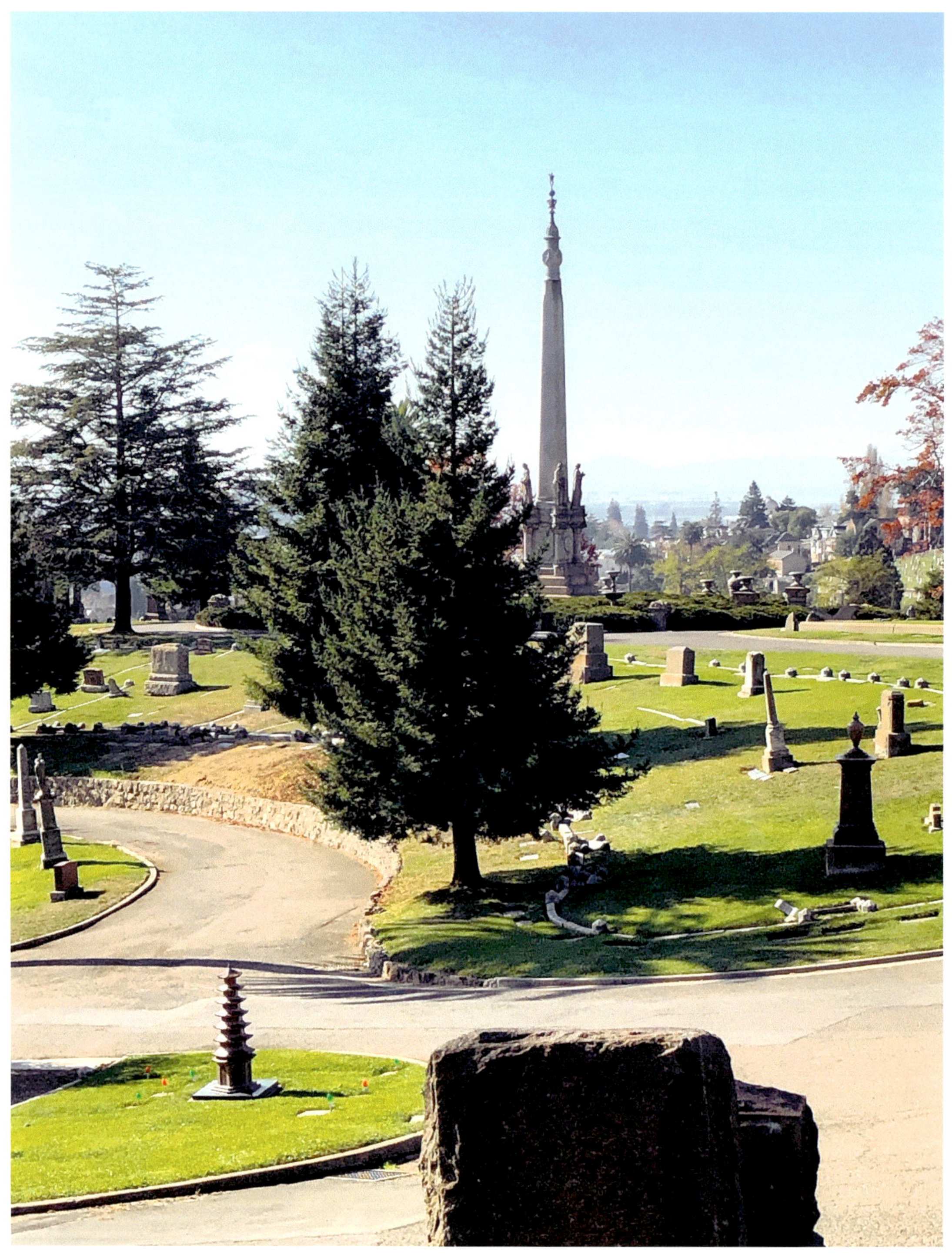

San Francisco seen from Mountain View.

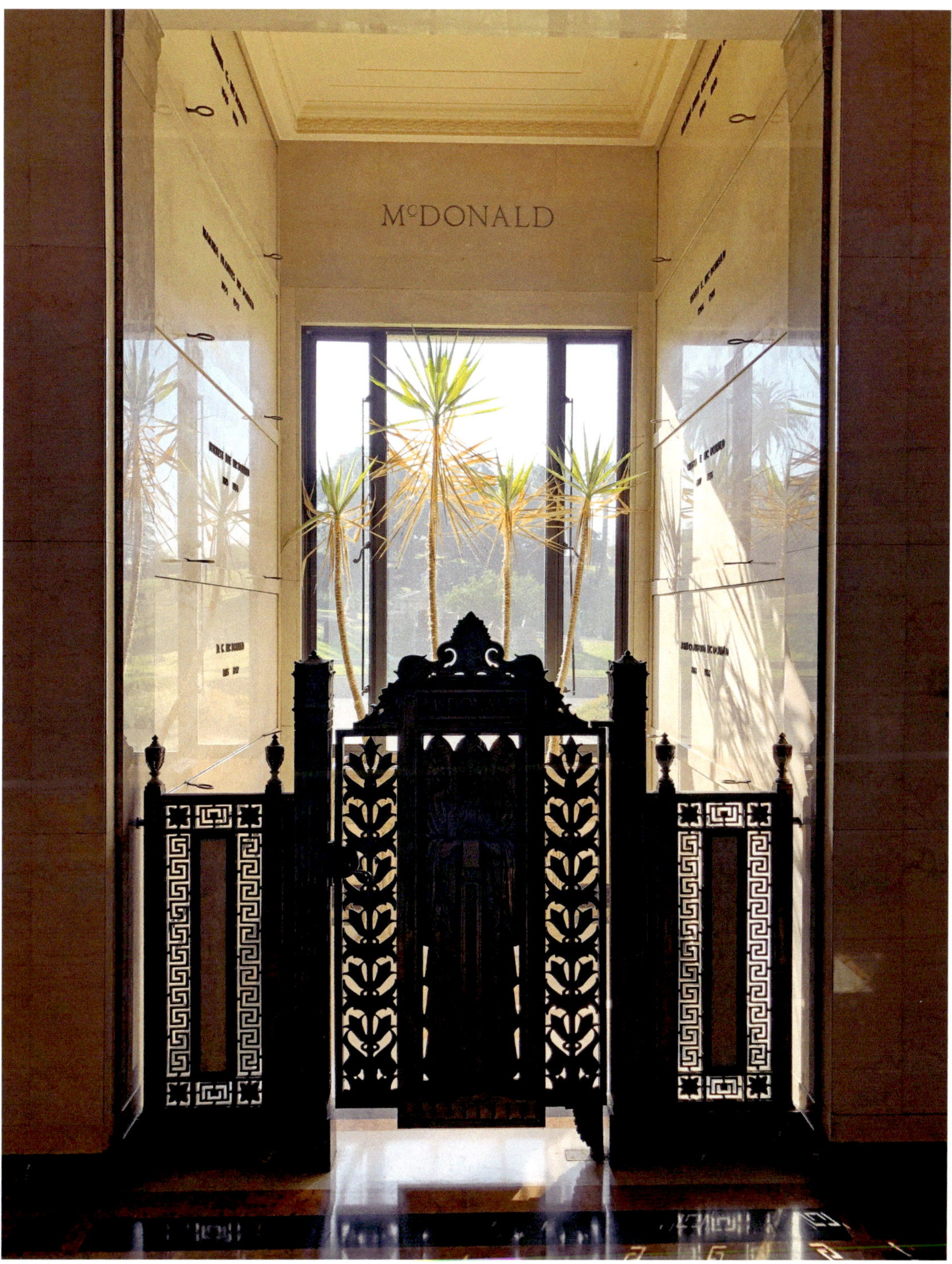


A sunny window in the mausoleum.

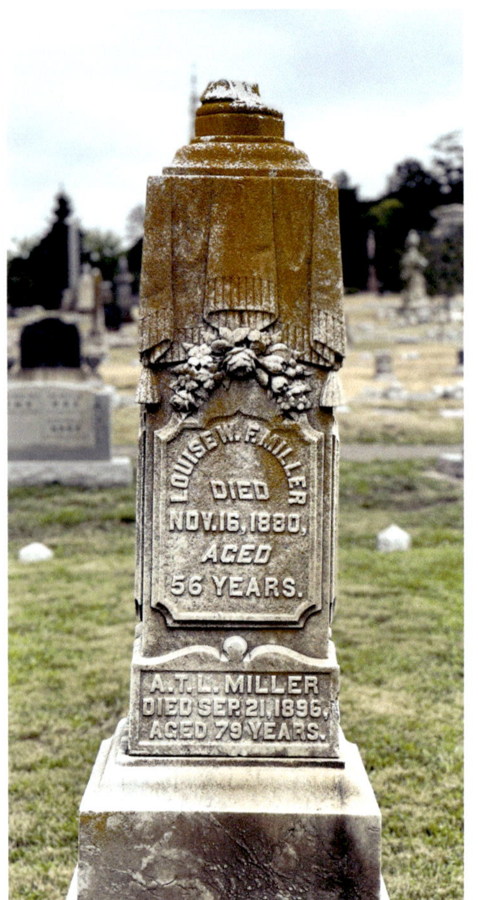

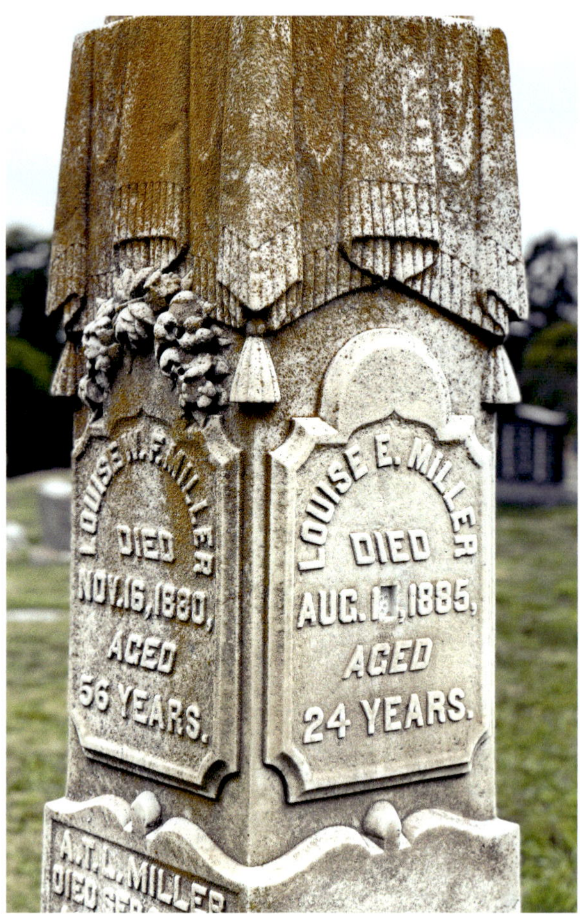

Gorgeous Victorian funeral symbolism: draped obelisk with tassels and floral garland.

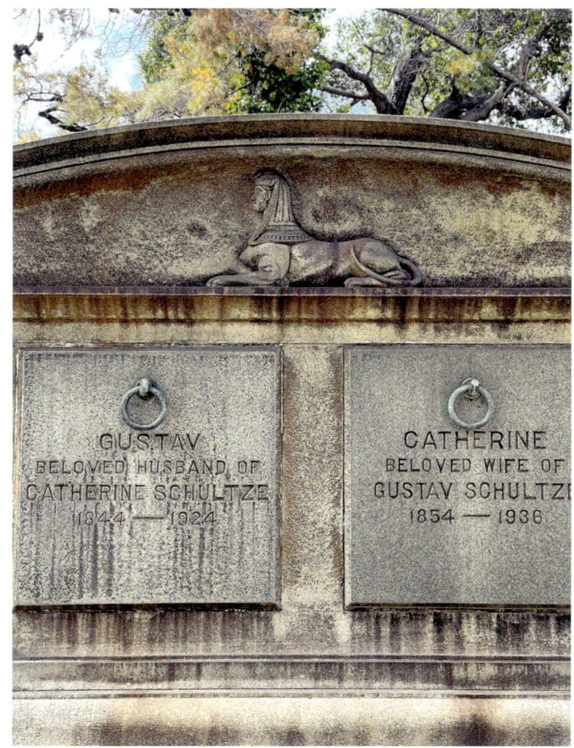

A family crypt.

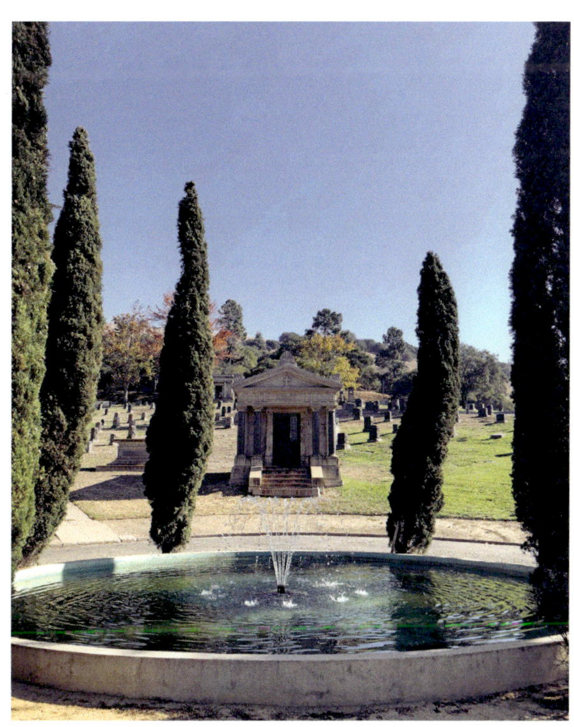

The fountain view.

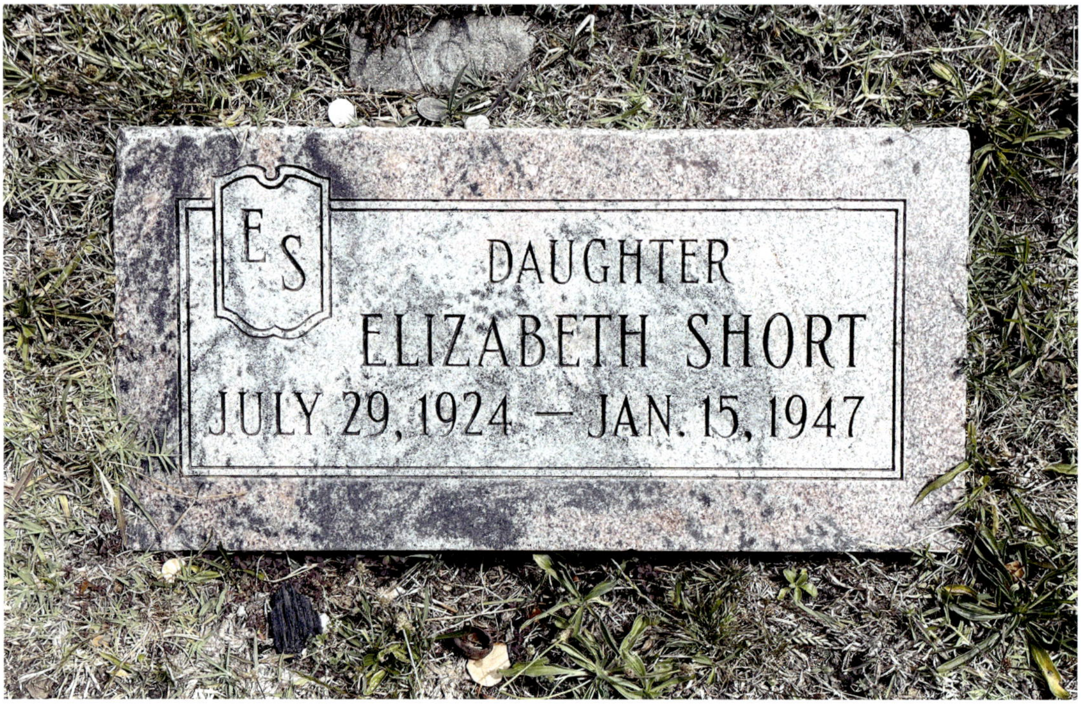

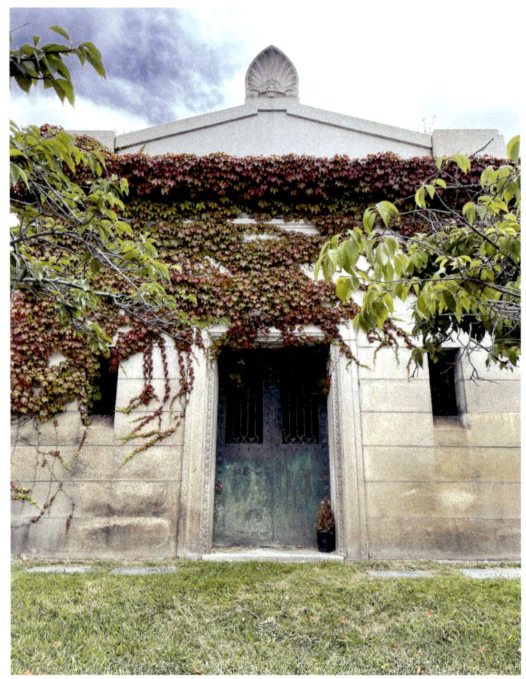

*Above:* The Black Dahlia, an adopted California daughter.

*Below:* Millionaire's Row.

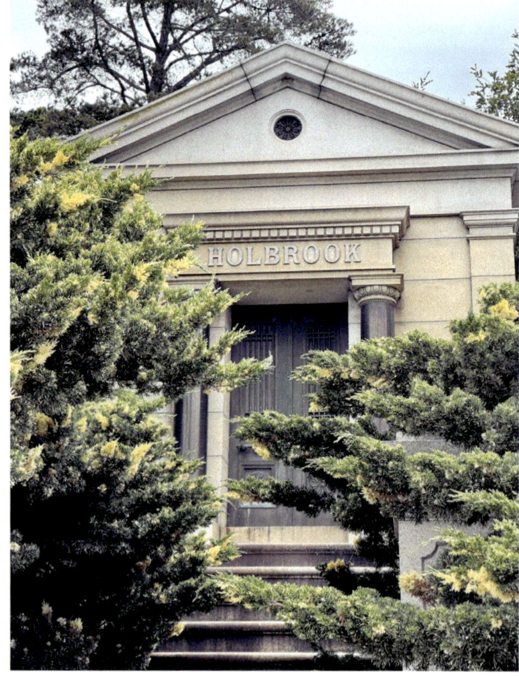

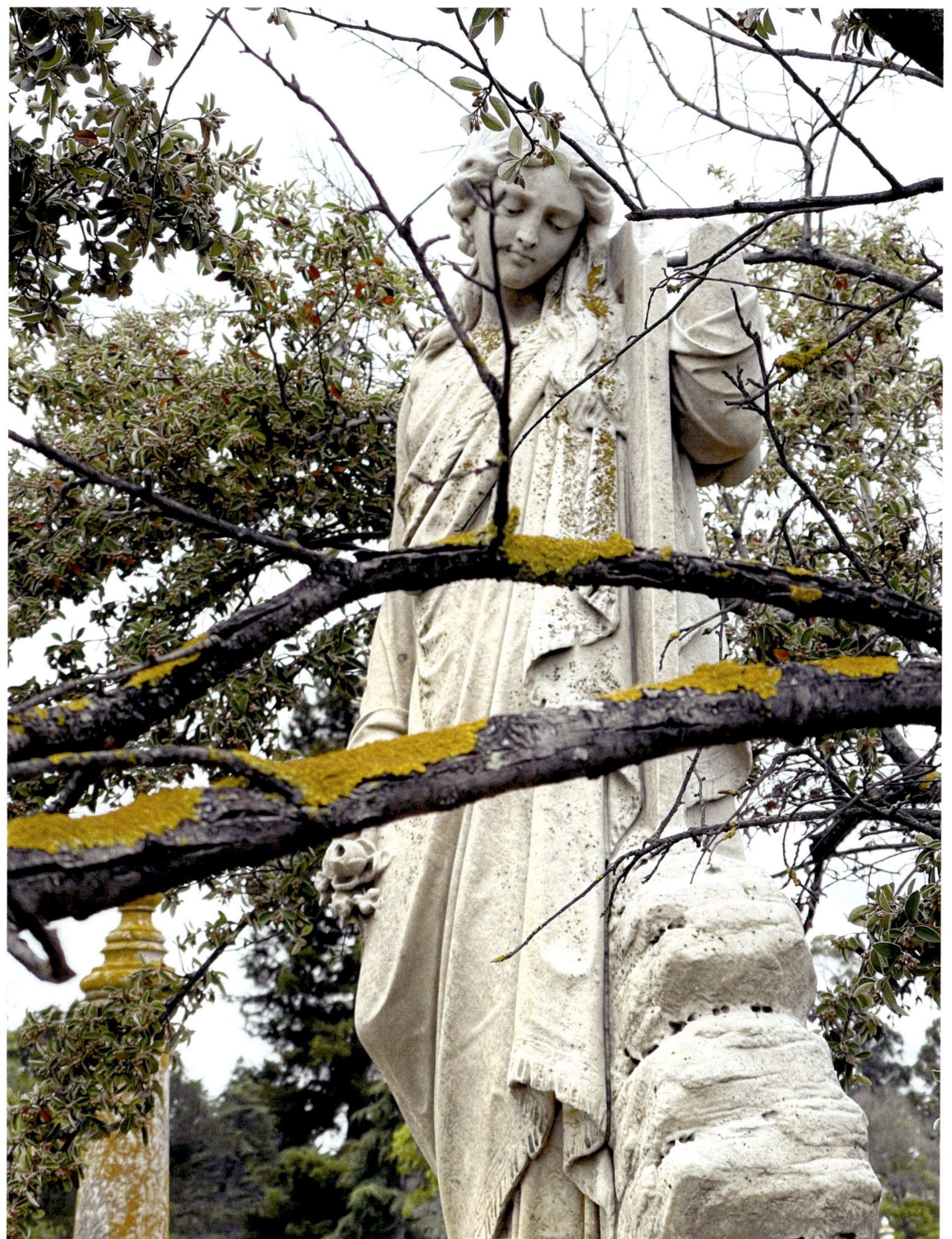

Seen through the trees.

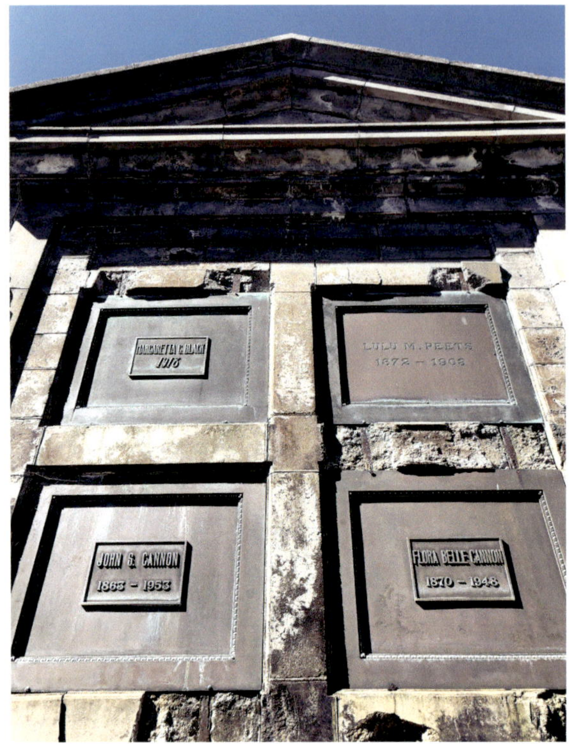

*Left:* A family crypt.

*Below:* Art Deco, Egyptian Revival details.

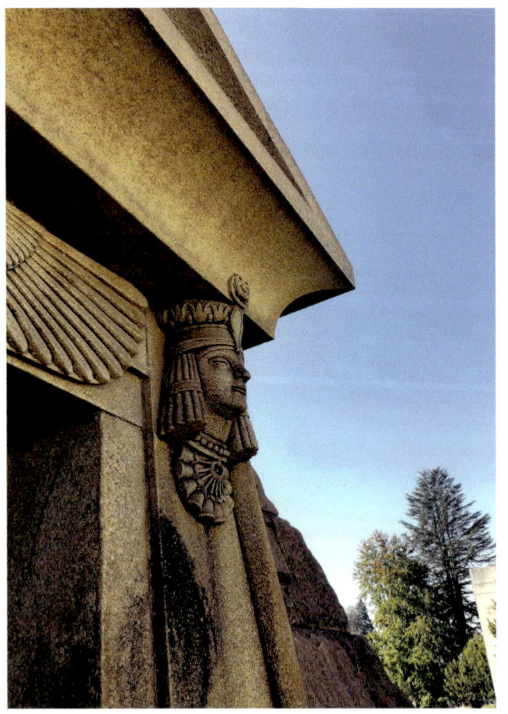

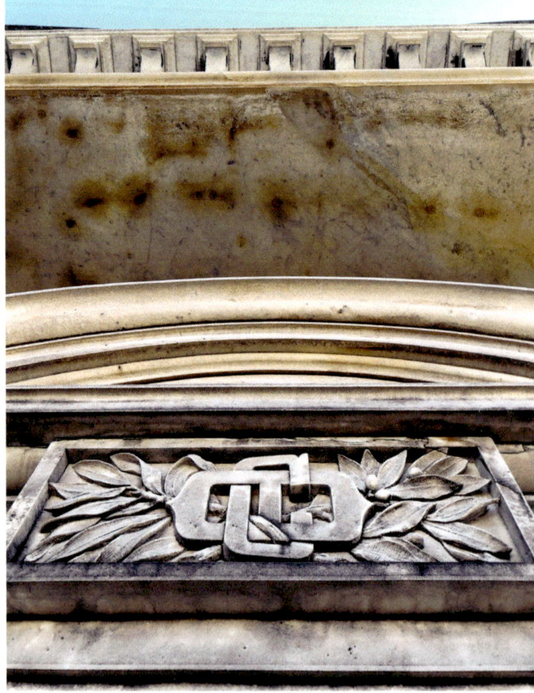

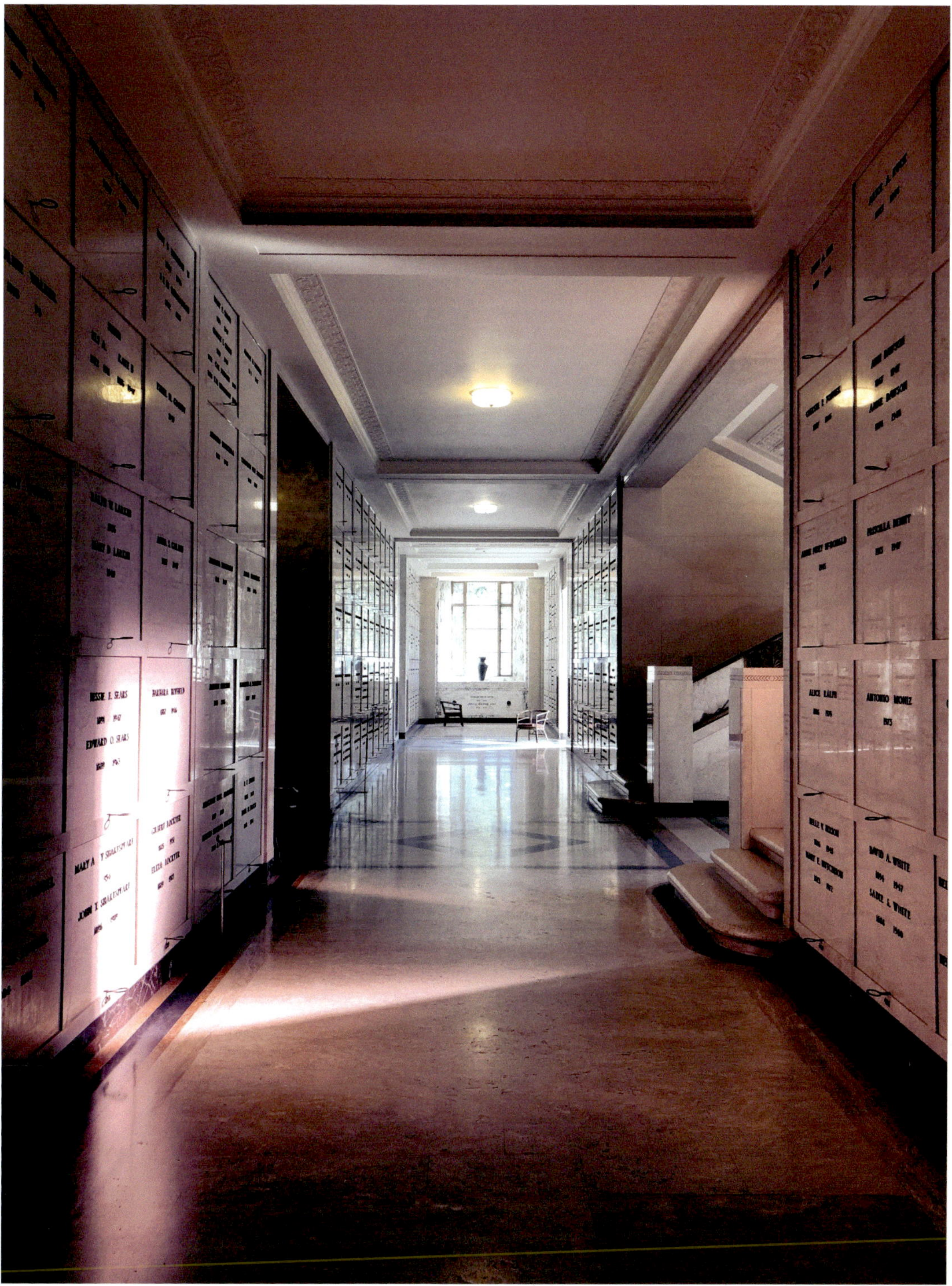

Purple haze.

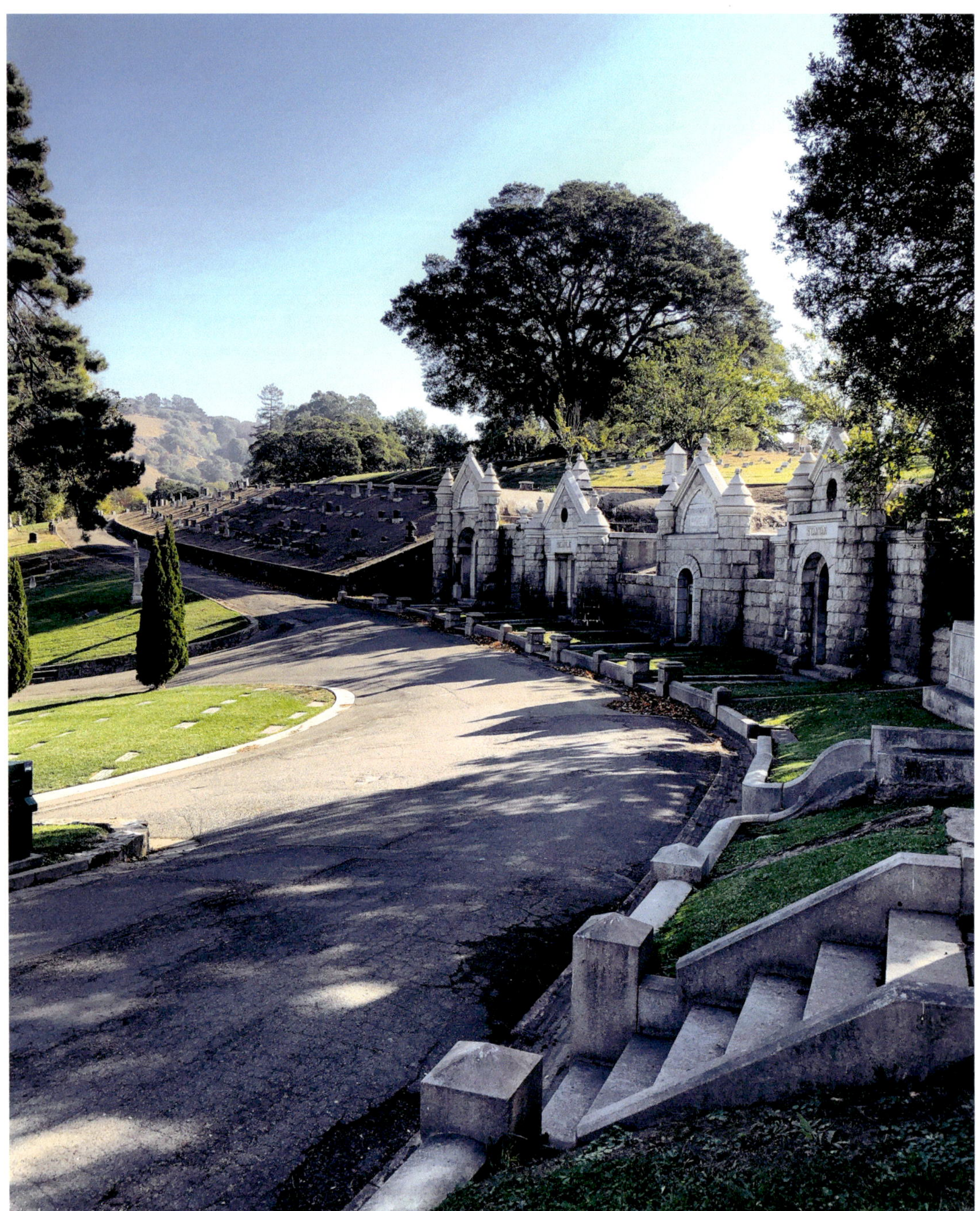

Last look on the hillside.

**3**

# THE CHAPEL OF THE CHIMES, OAKLAND

The Chapel of the Chimes, just outside Mountain View's gates, was first established as a columbarium and crematorium in 1909. After a period of disrepair and damage, architect Julia Morgan, the designer of Hearst Castle and the first woman to ever become a certified architect in the U.S., was called in for a significant renovation. The result is absolutely stunning. Still an active funeral home, the Chapel of the Chimes is breathtakingly beautiful. It's easy to see why people refer to it as a "library of souls."

I've visited the Chapel of the Chimes many times, but my first was on an extremely hot day during the pandemic. Walking the still halls of the mausoleum with a face mask on is not necessarily recommended, so the rooms with open skylights were a welcome respite to the still, solid air that fills its halls. Just as I left that Chapel that day, a funeral cortege was pulling in. As I stepped outside, still under the Chapel's awning, there was a deafening thunder clap and a sudden rainstorm.

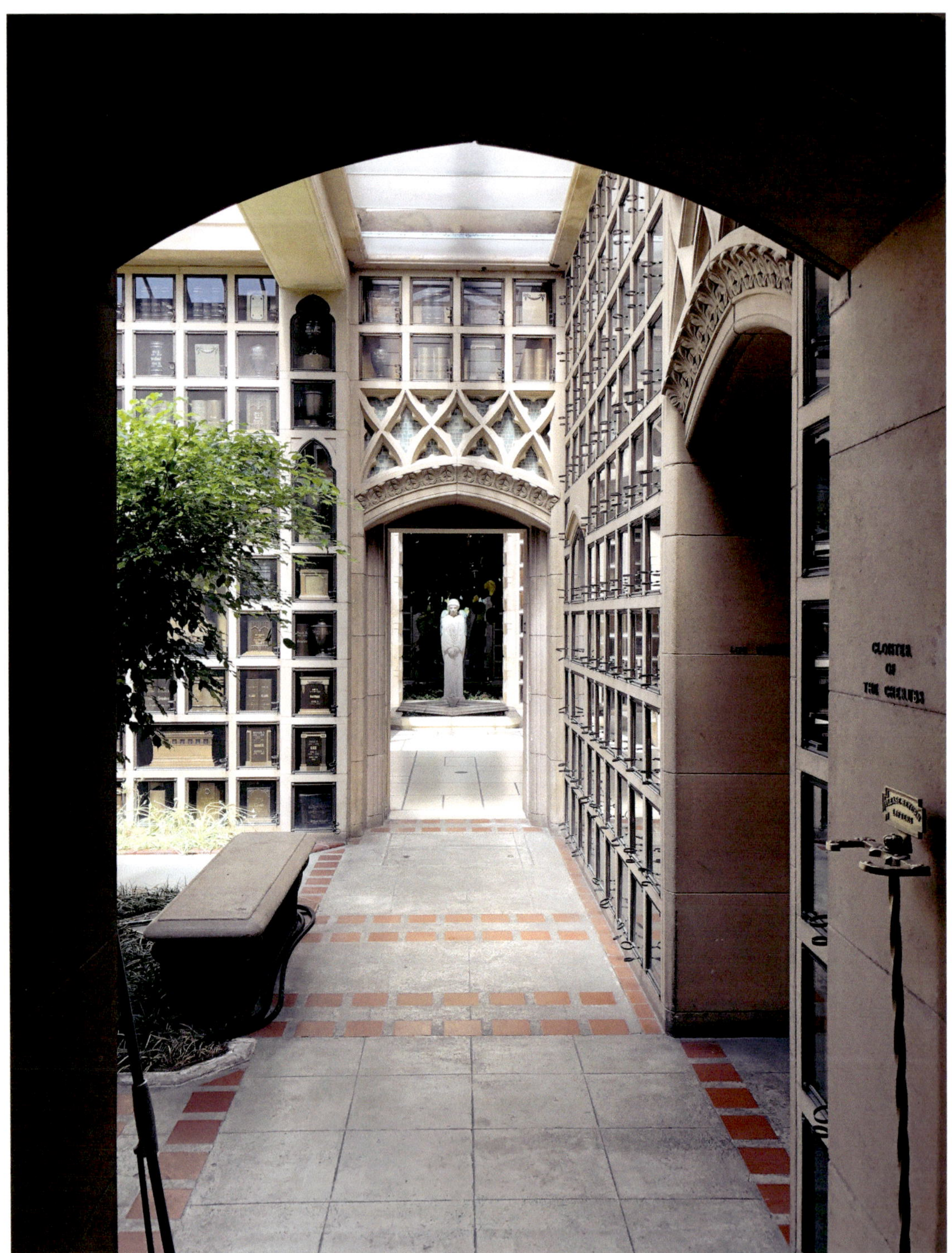

A welcoming angel at the Chapel of the Chimes.

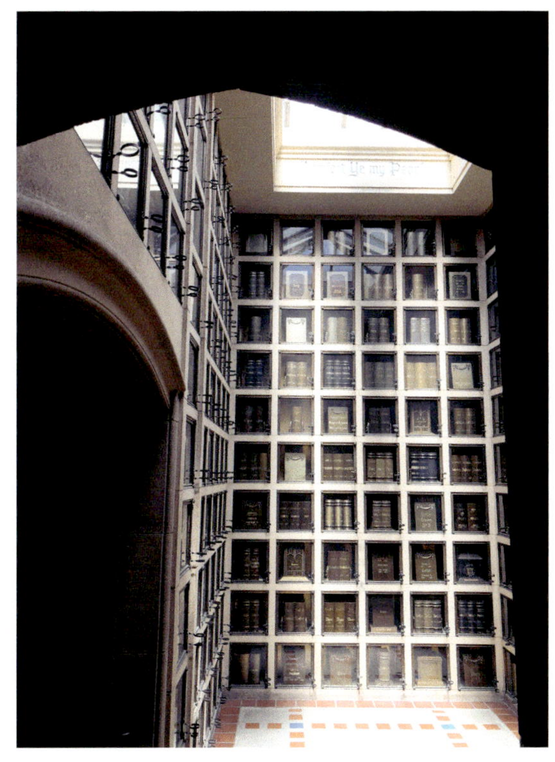

The library of souls.

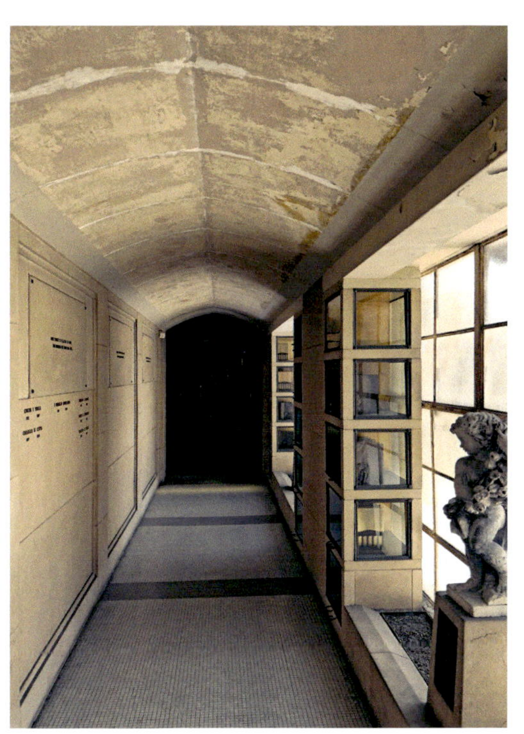

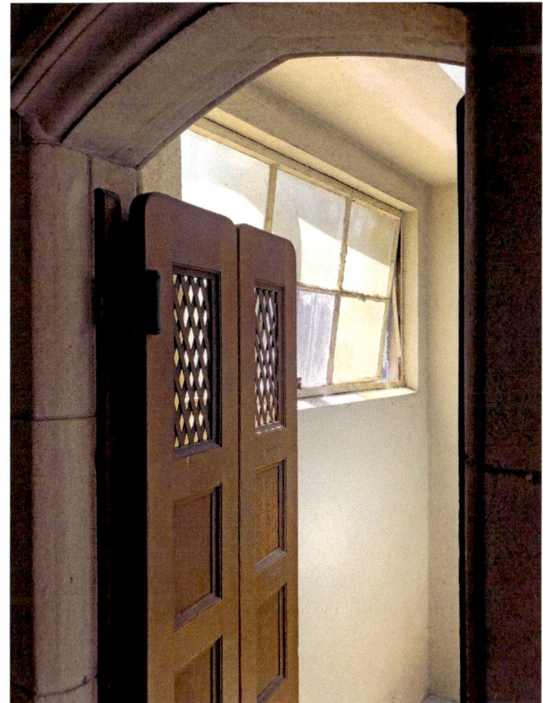

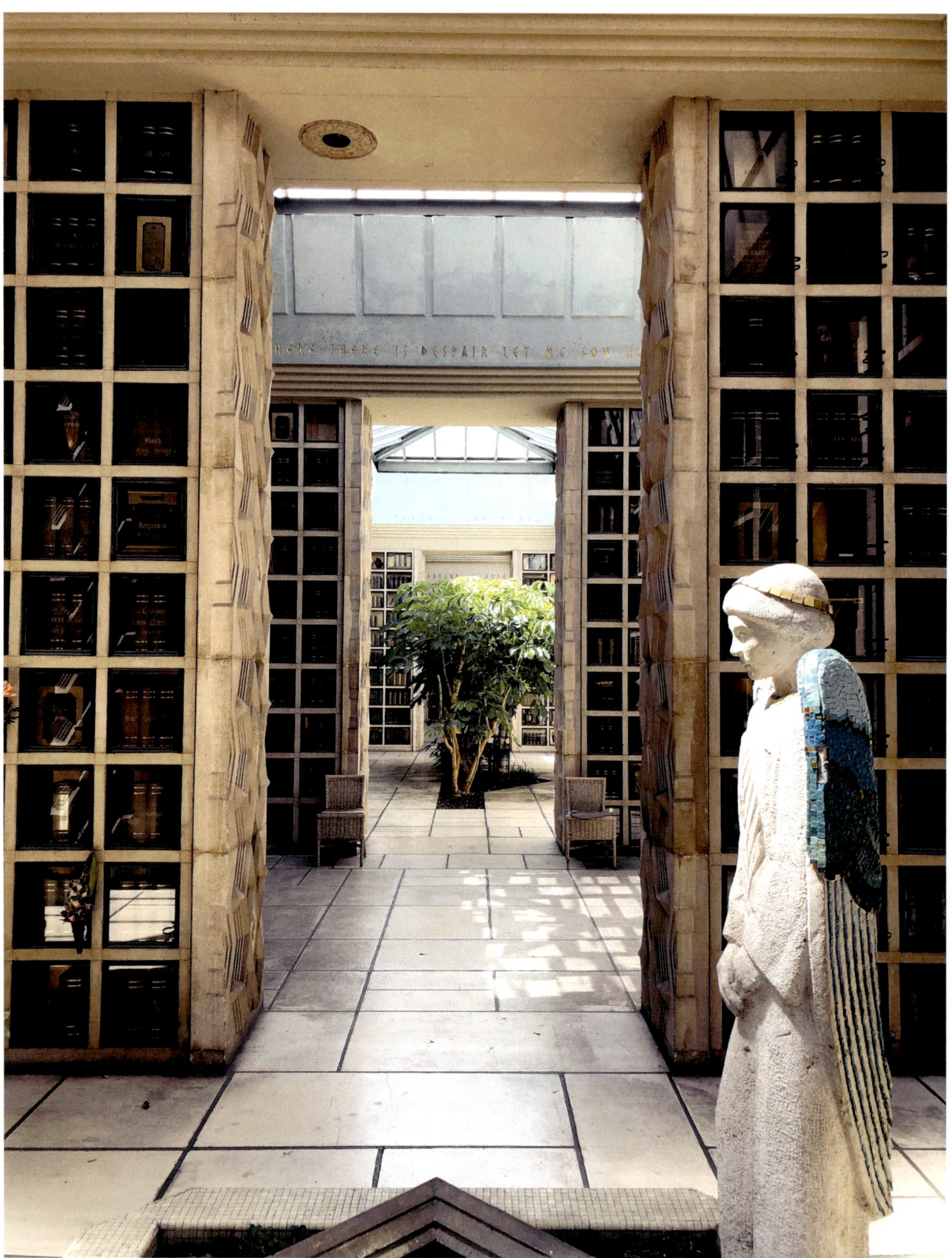

More views of the angel with her blue mosaic wings.

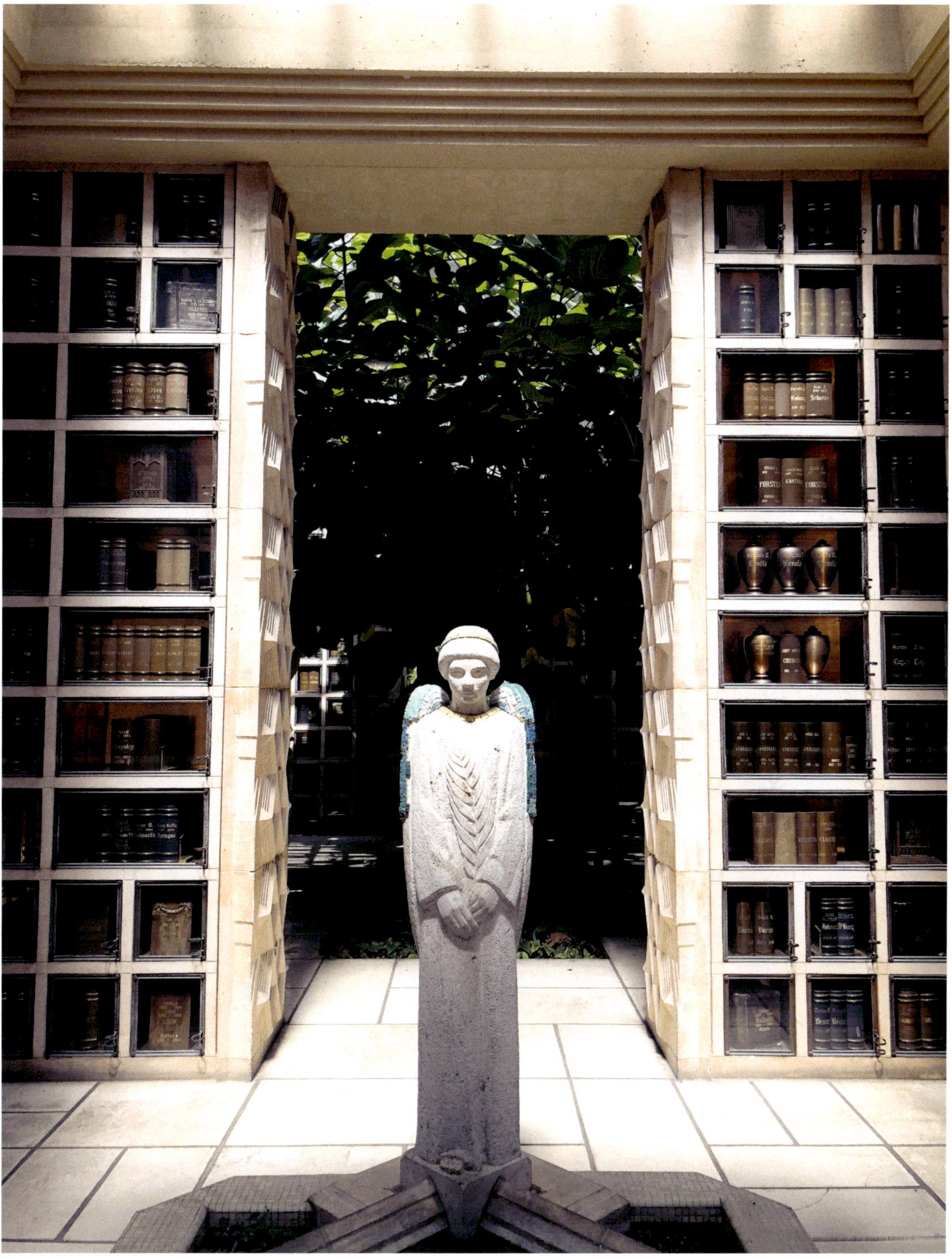

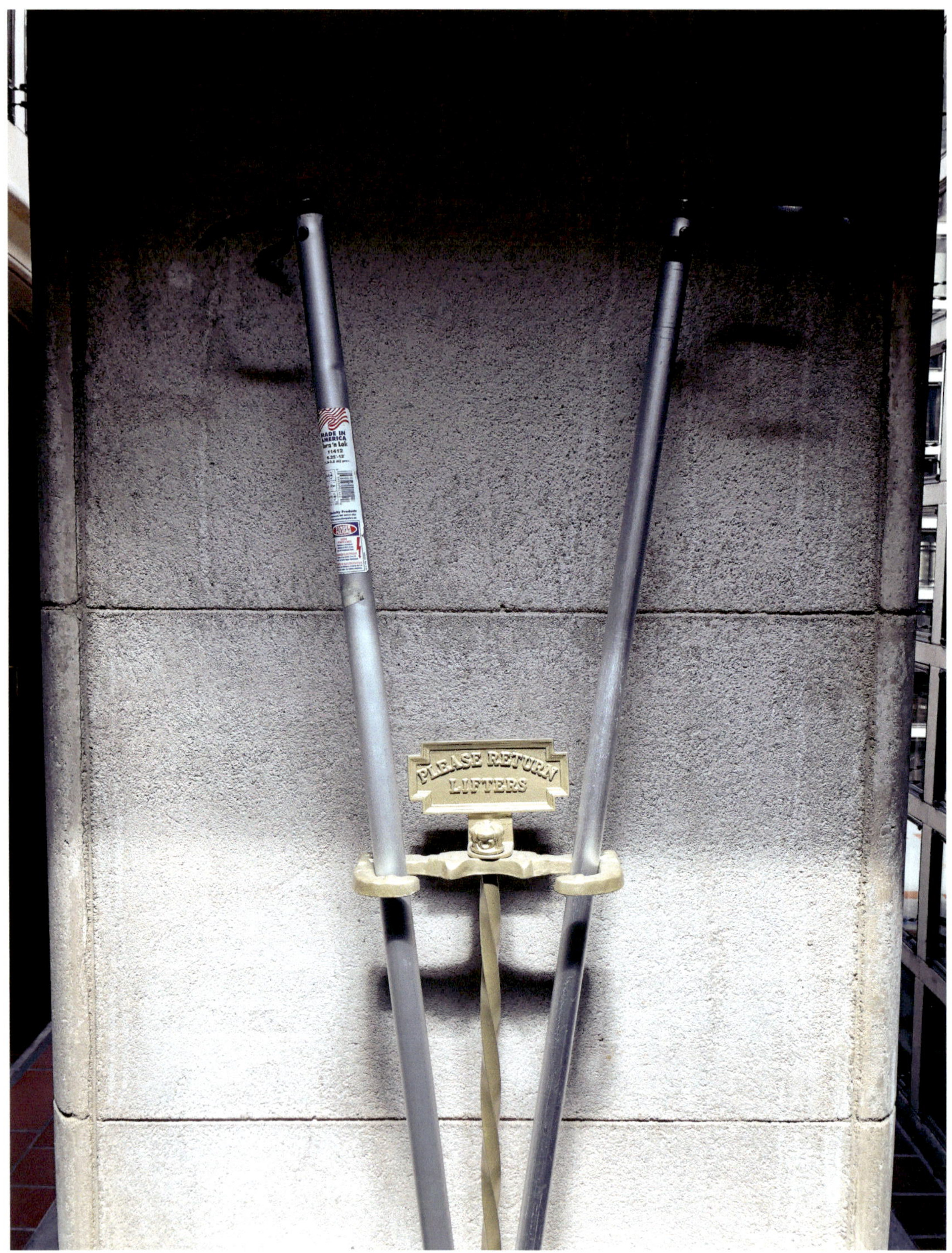


Lifters for niche vases.

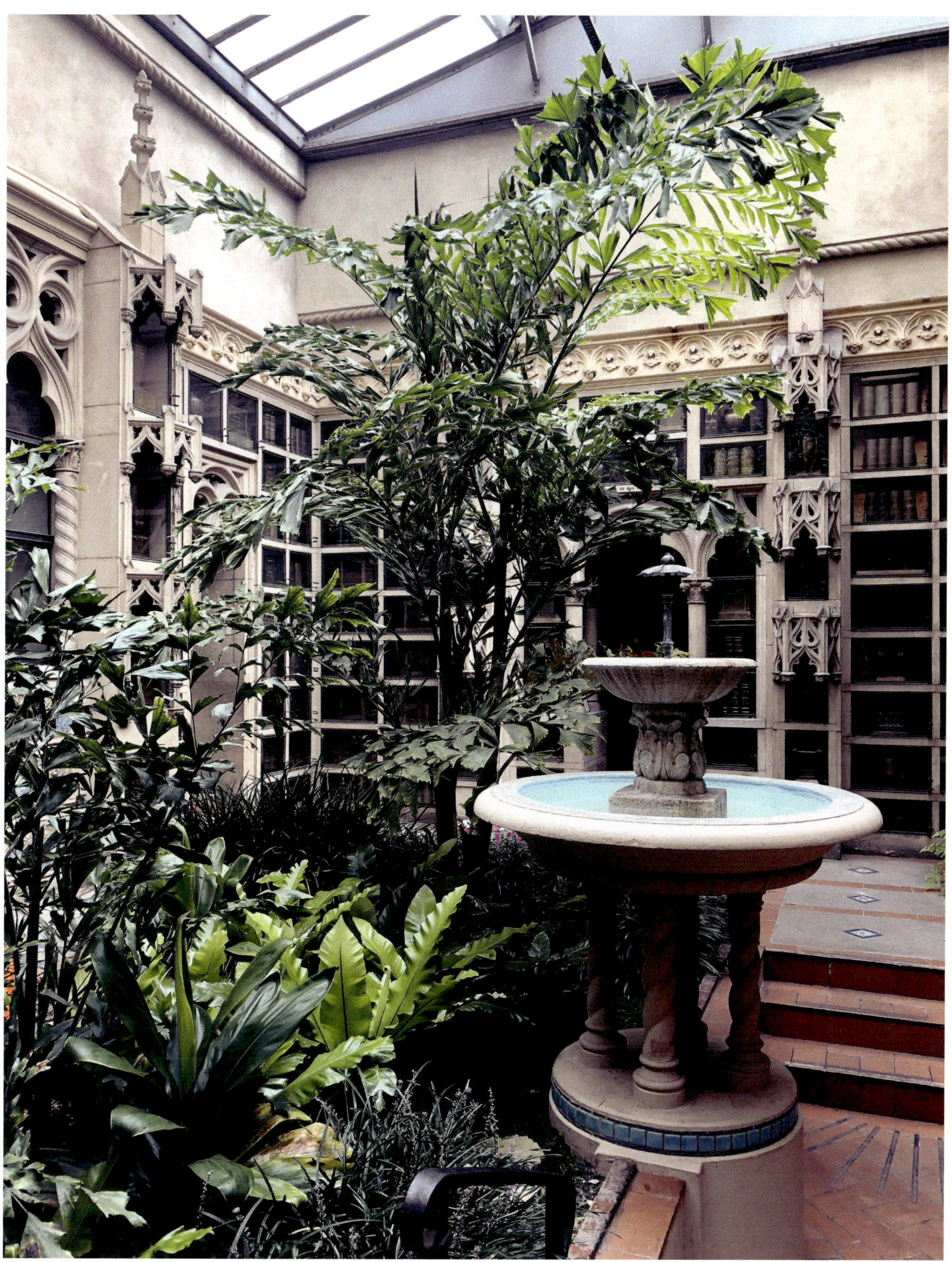

Courtyard views.

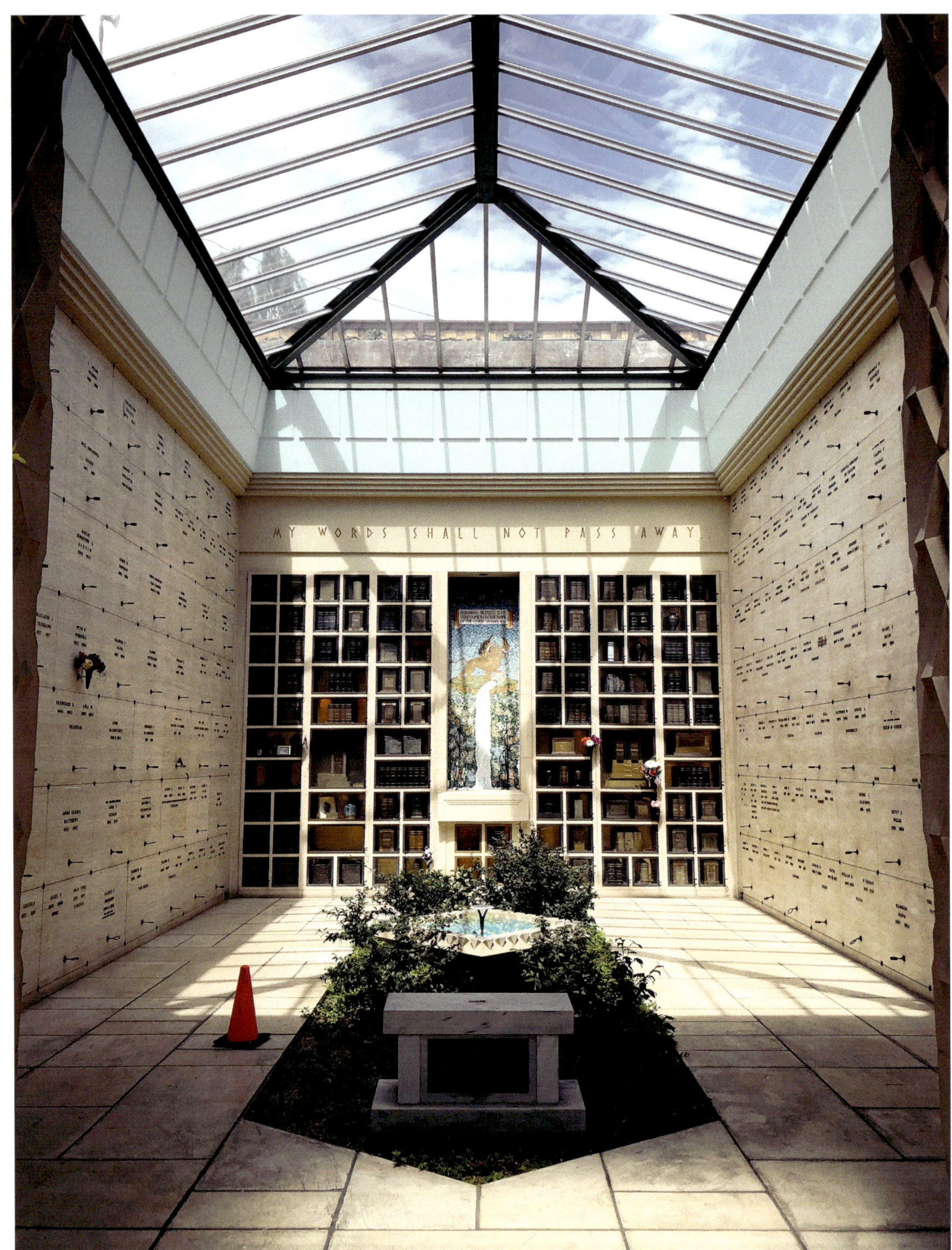

Courtyard views.

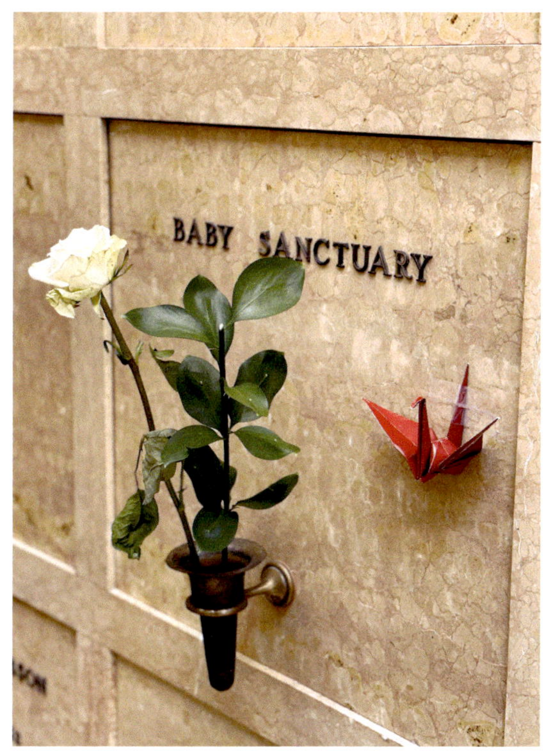


Babyland.

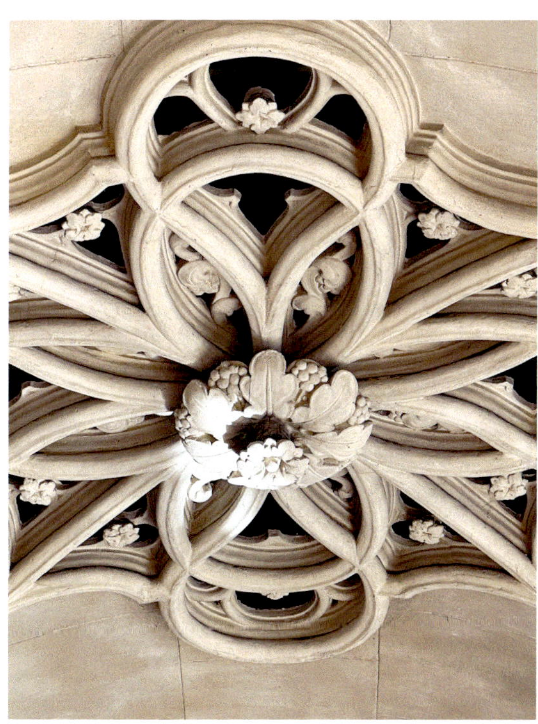

The Gothic-style ceiling.

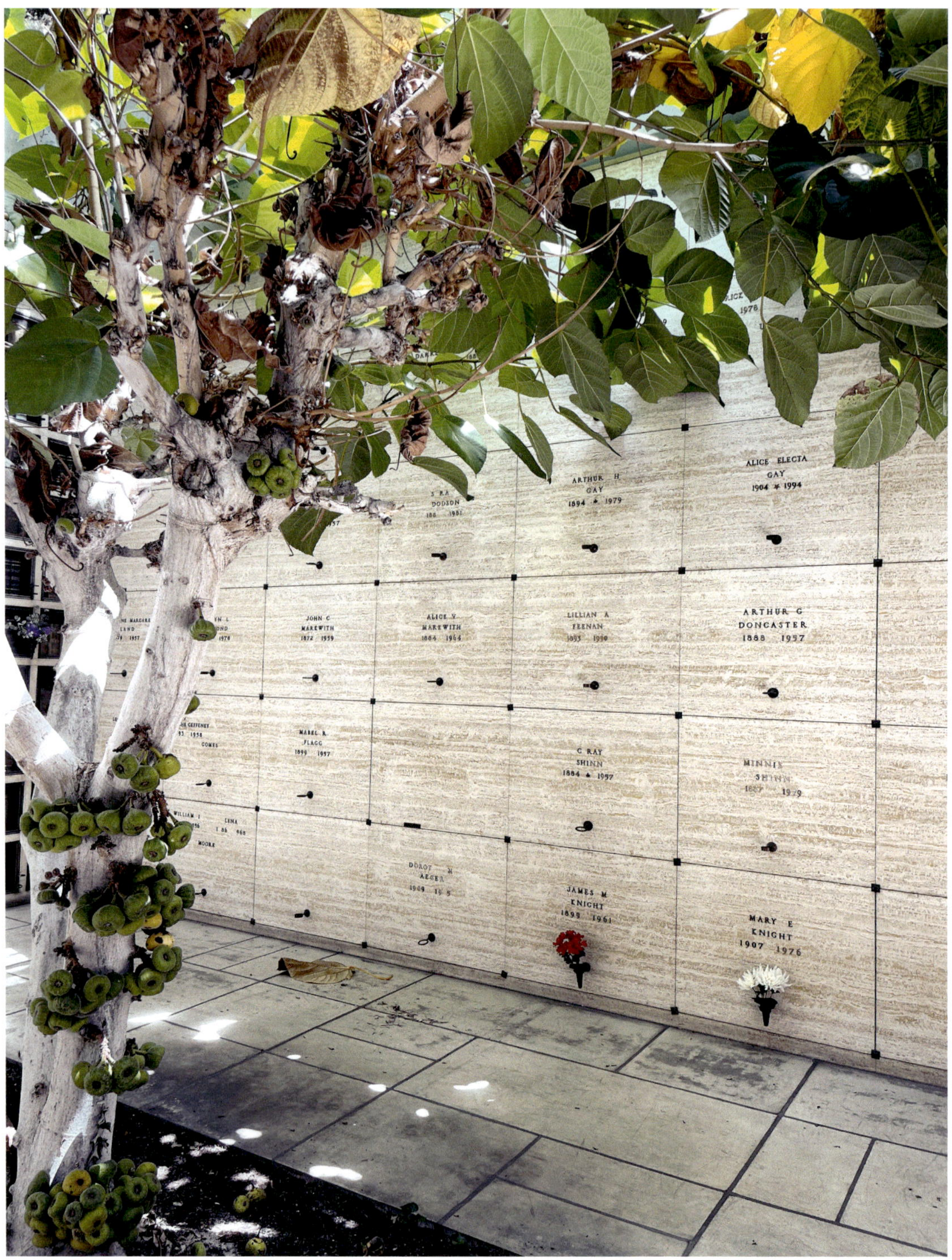

Gorgeous crypt atrium with tree.

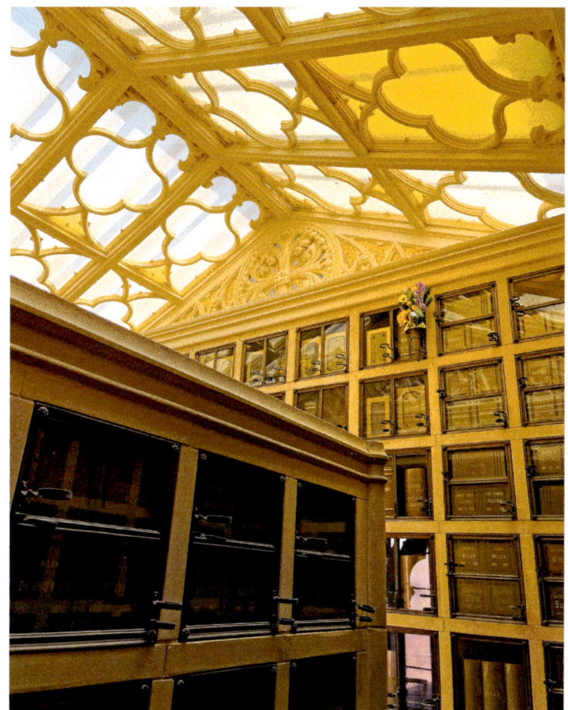

Filtered sunlight.

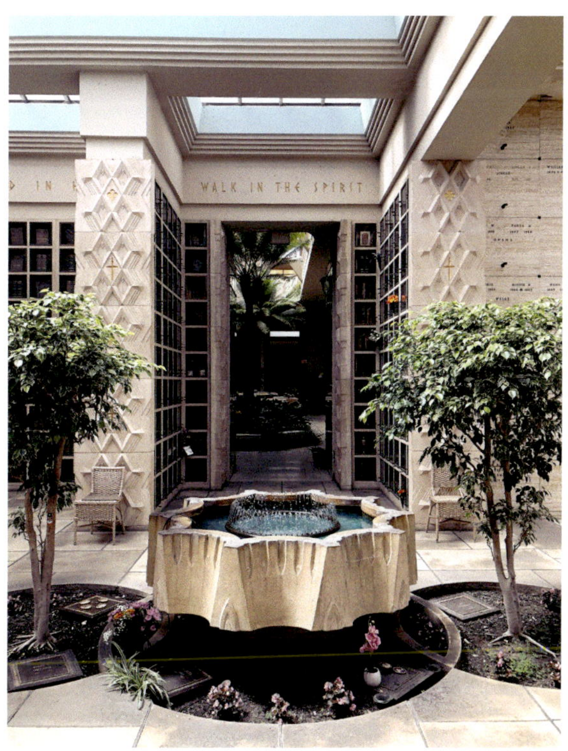



Walk in the spirit.

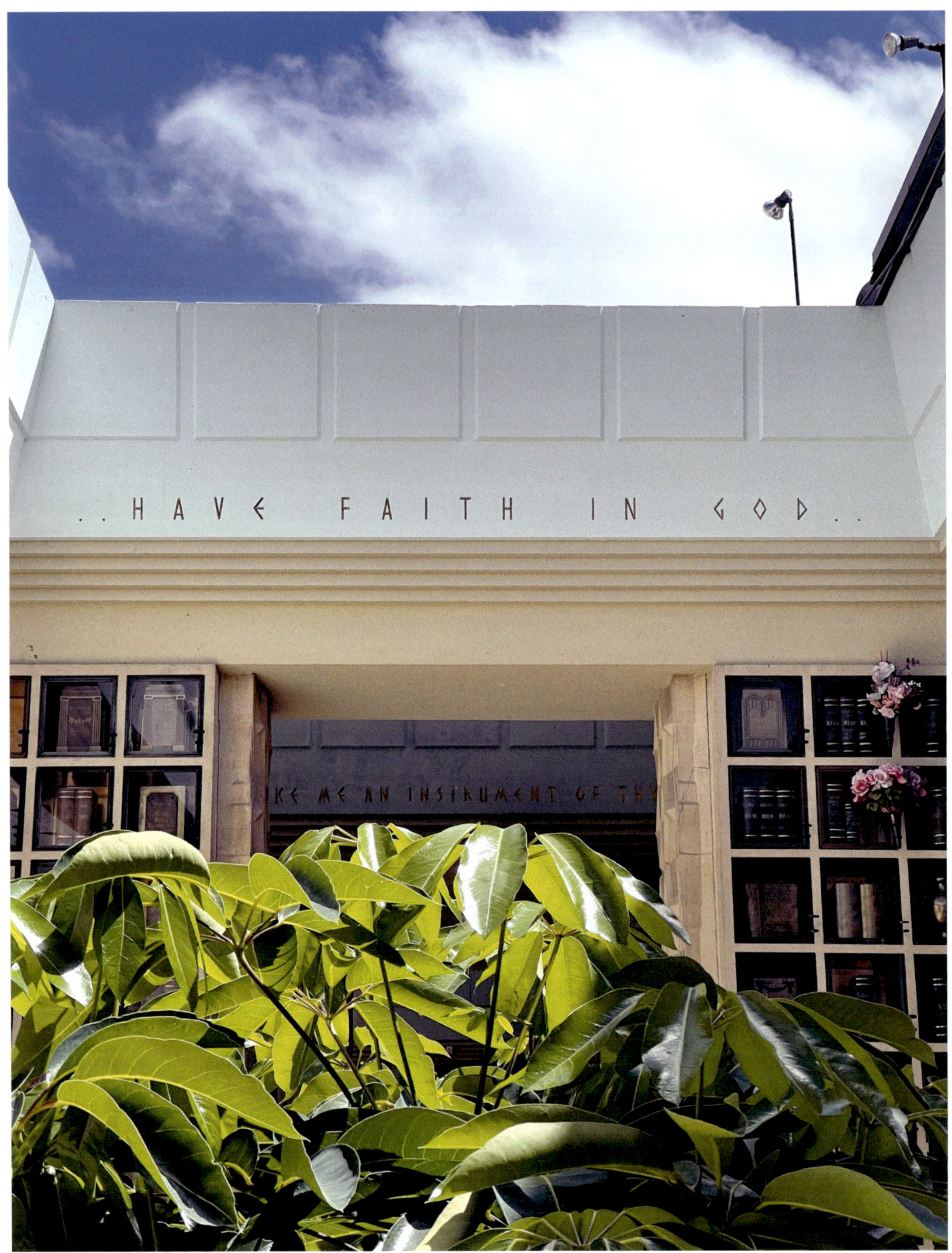


Have faith in God.

# 4

# SUNSET VIEW CEMETERY, EL CERRITO

Sunset View, with its sweeping views of the Bay, is a cemetery that lives up to its name. Founded in the early 1900s for the growing community in the Berkeley Hills, Sunset View gained a stylish mortuary and chapel in mid-century and is still an active cemetery with a big, beautiful mausoleum at the top of its hill.

Many people in the community use Sunset View for recreation. During visits it is common to see the living out for a walk with their dogs or jogging up to the top of the hill. On my first visit, near the cemetery's open hills at the back of the mausoleum, there was a father playing frisbee with his son. Inside the mausoleum, there was a virtual Spanish church service going on. As I toured the bottom floor of the mausoleum, I could hear the minister's sermon droning through the empty marble halls.

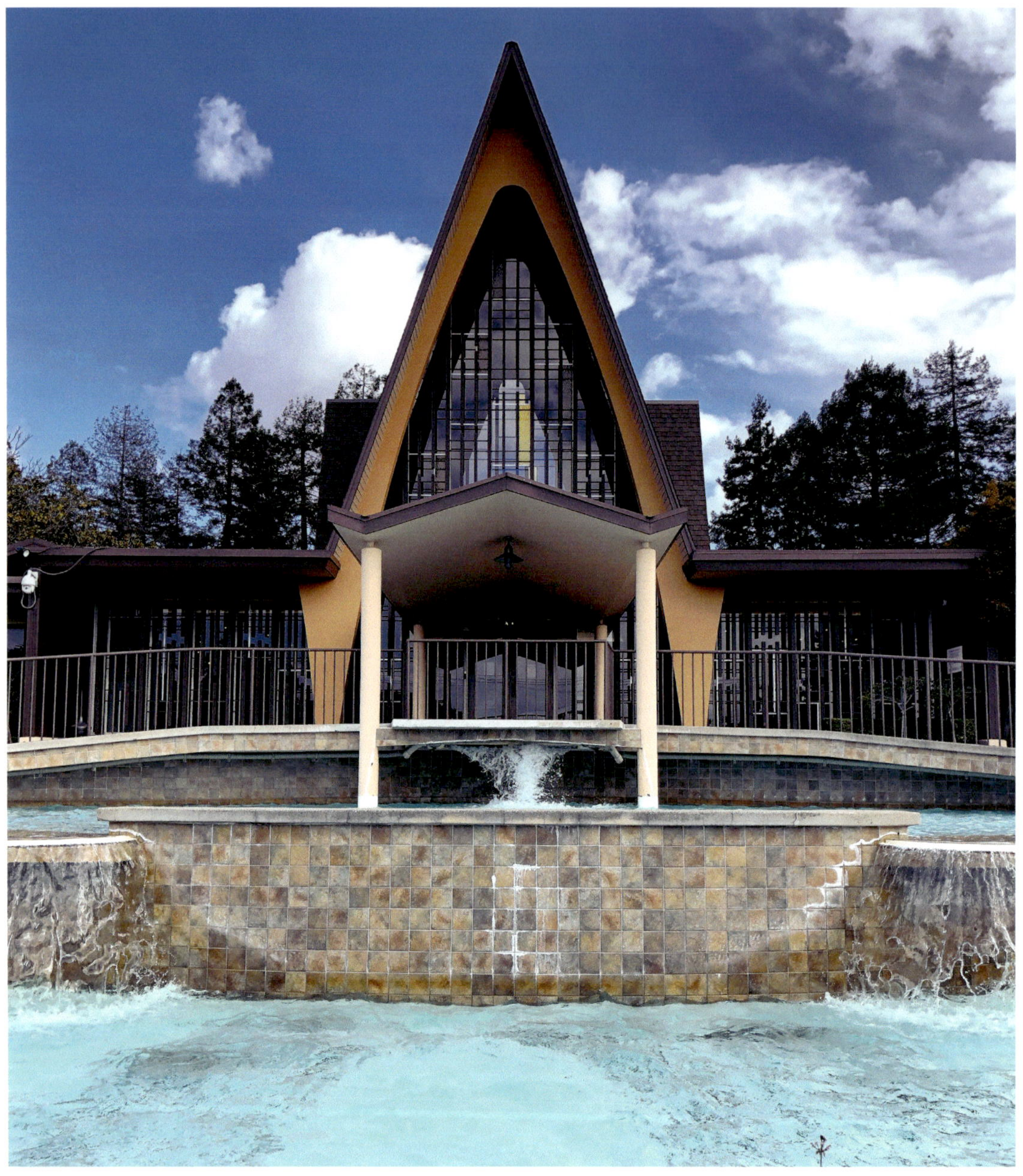

Sunset View's gorgeous mid-century modern mortuary and fountain.

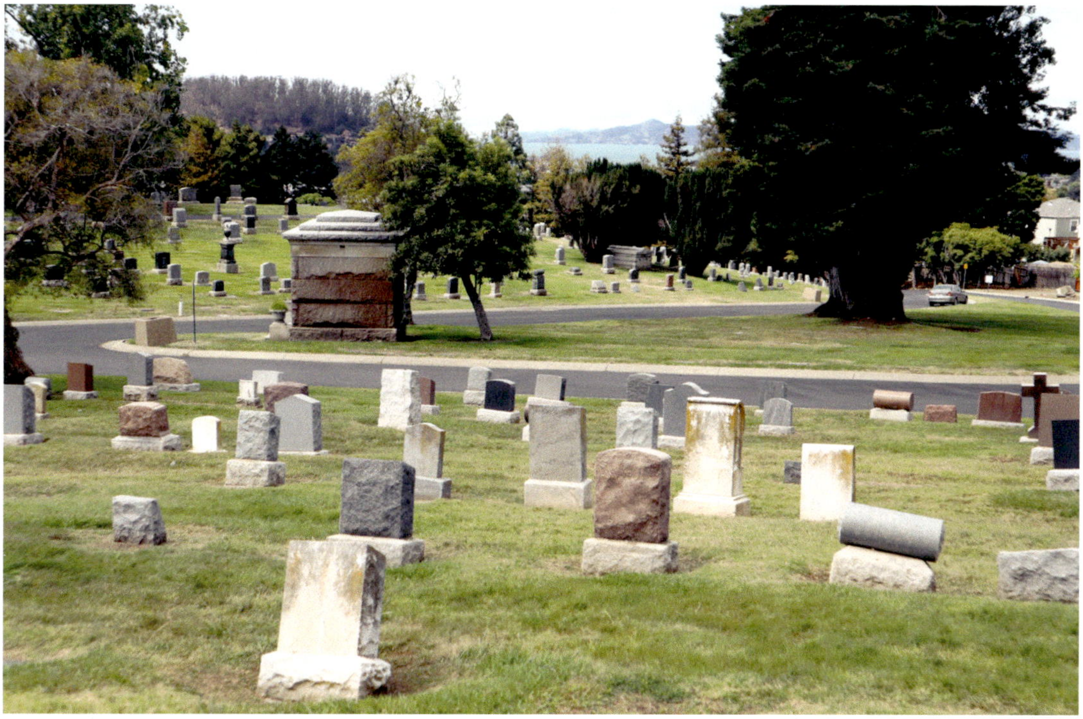

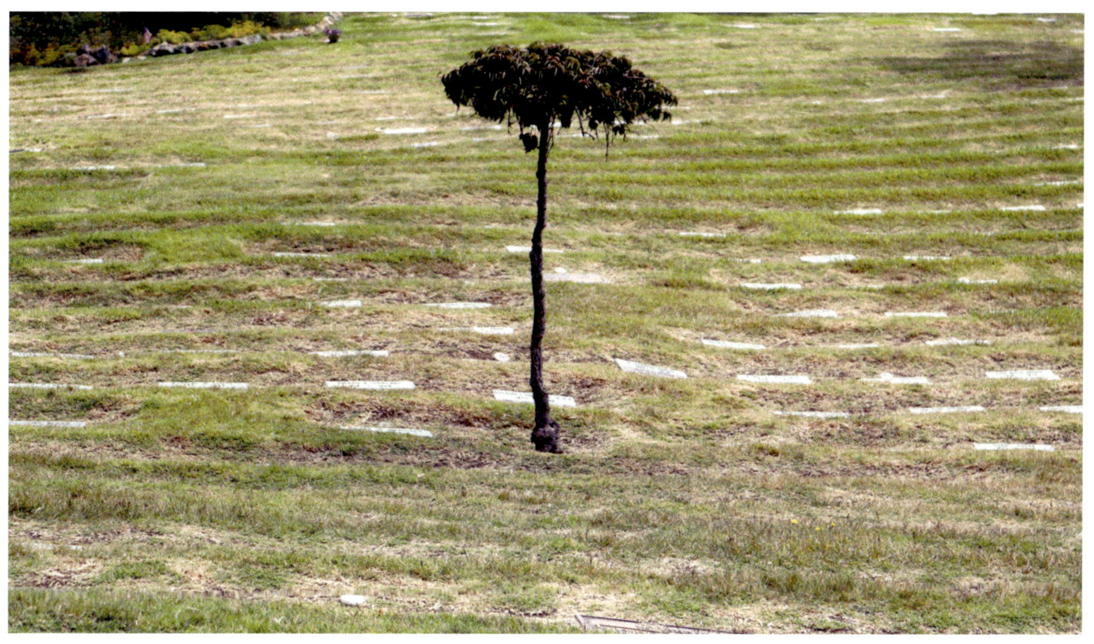

View of the Bay from Sunset View.

A lone tree.

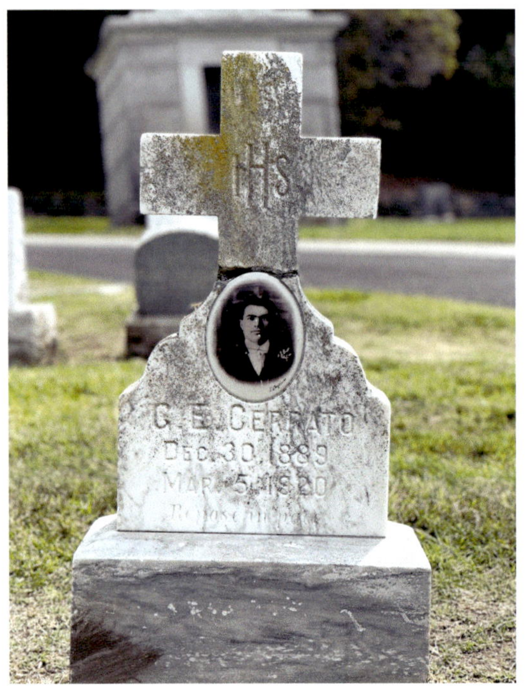

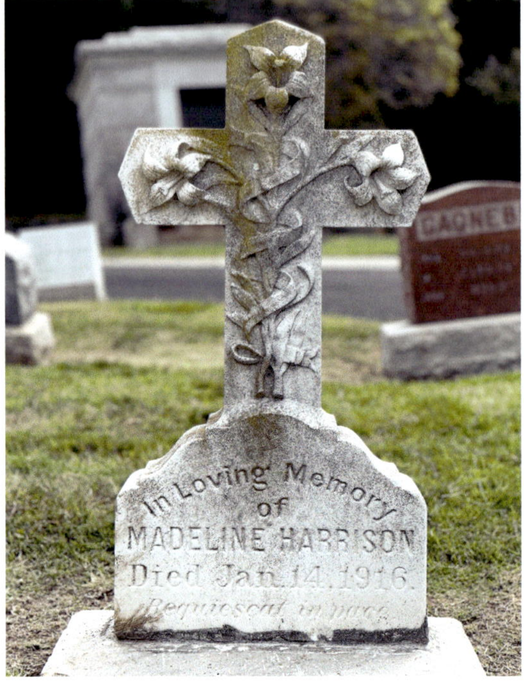

Repose in pace.

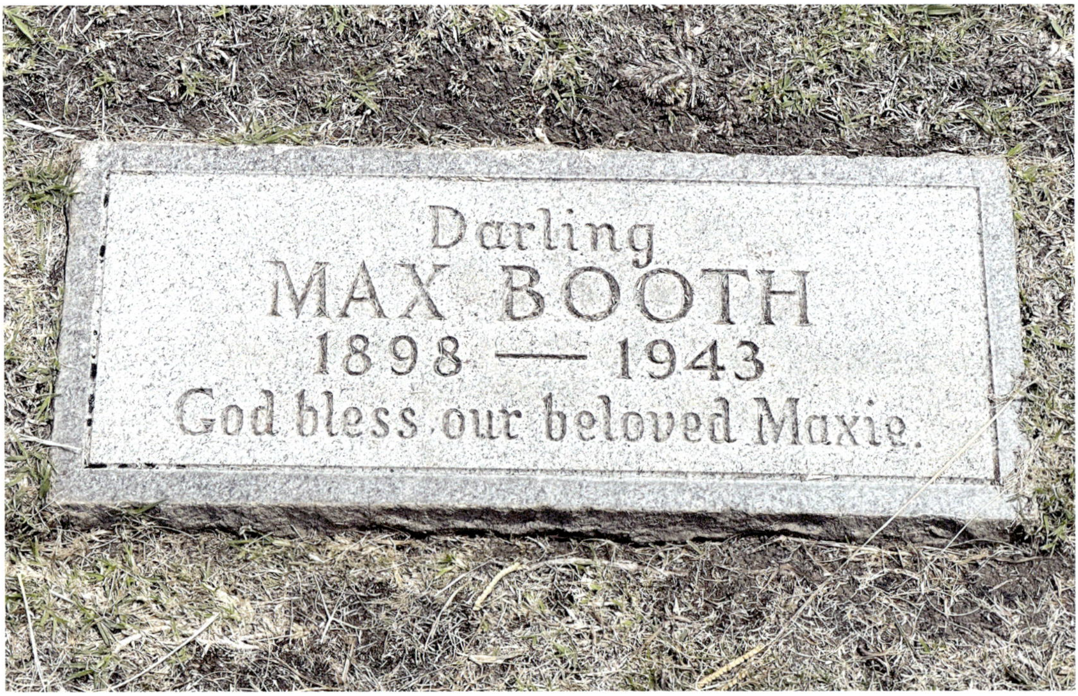

Darling Maxie.

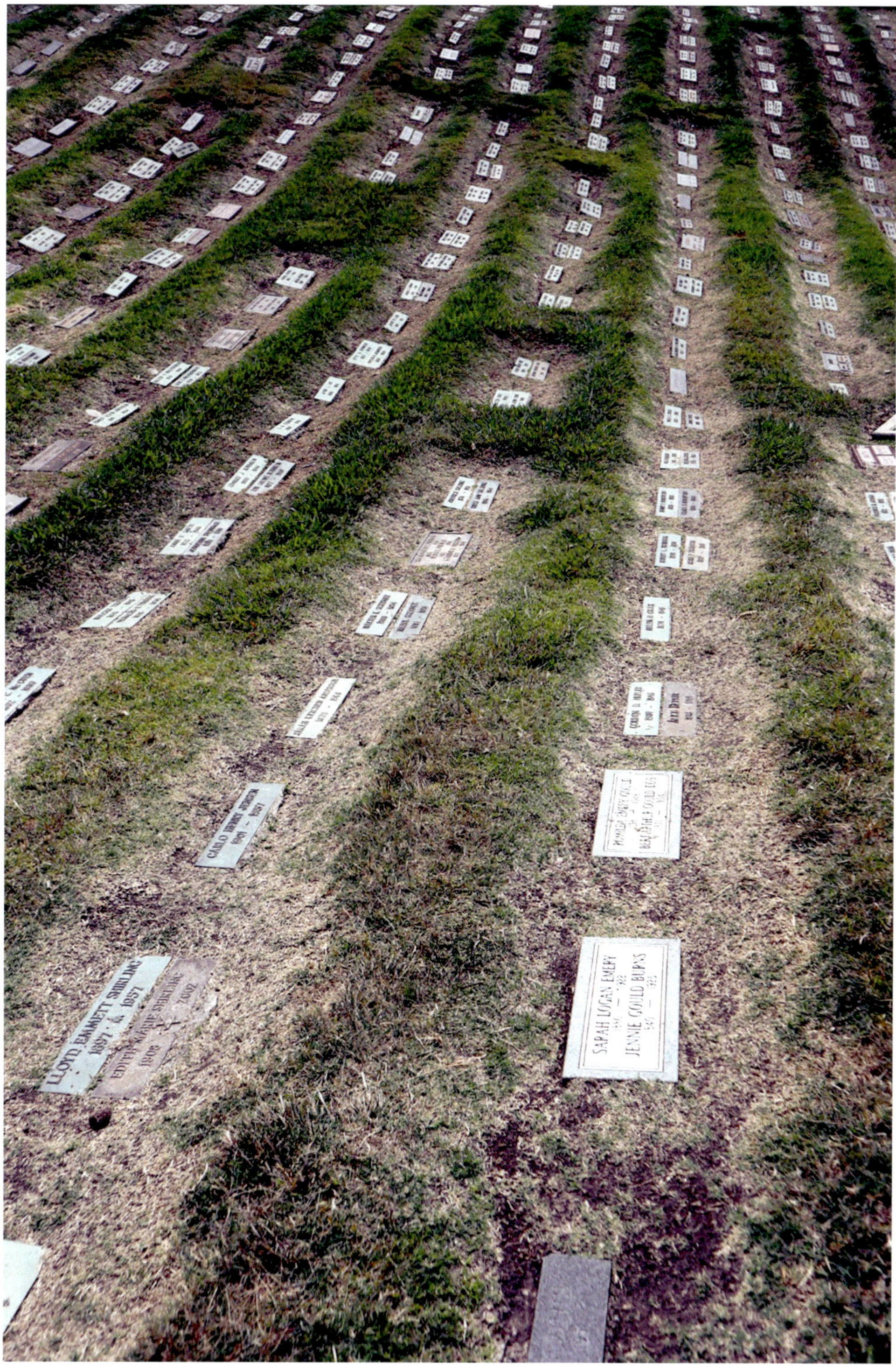

Rolling hills of the memorial park.

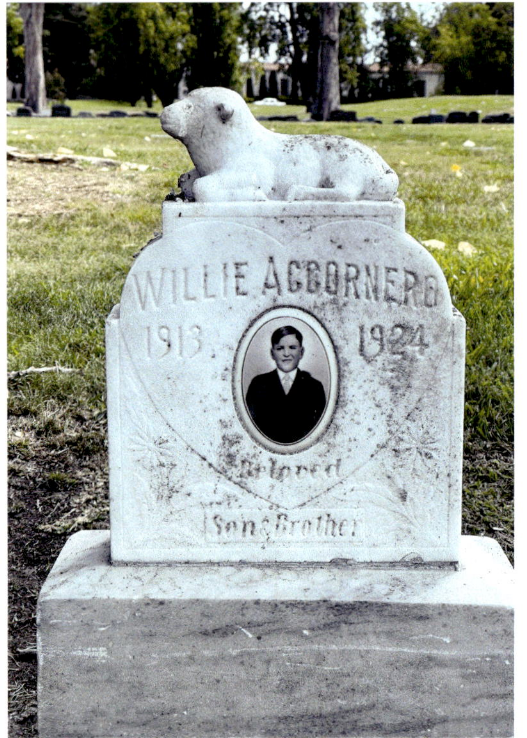

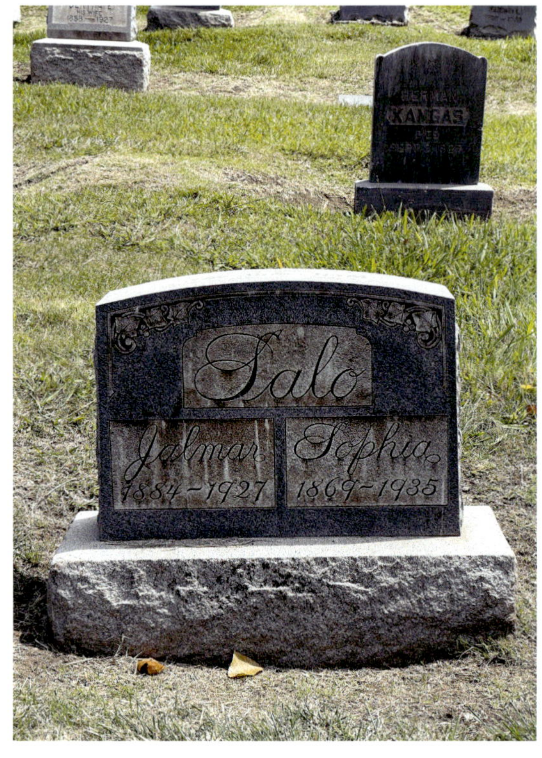

*These pages:* Permanent residents.

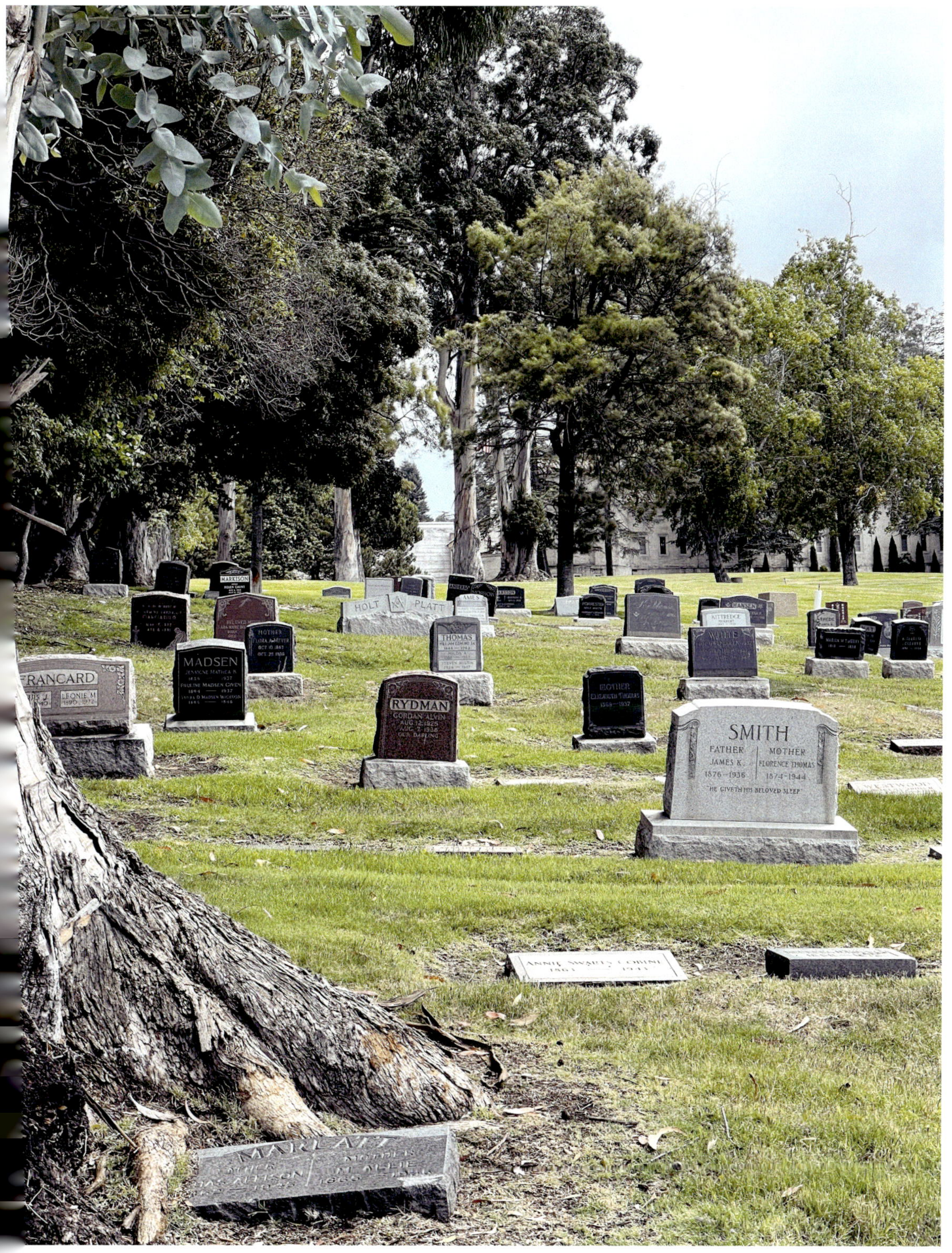

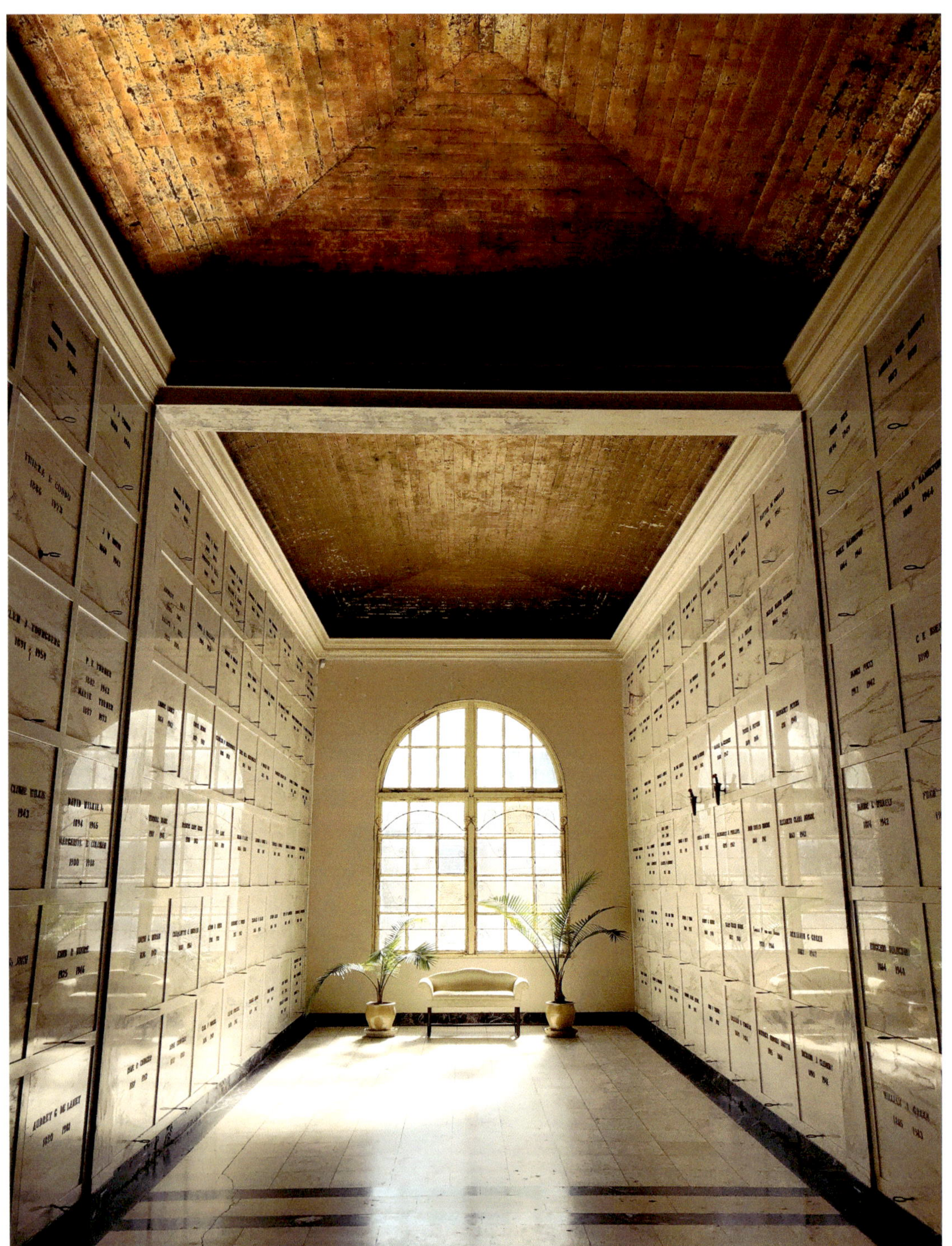

*These pages:* Sunset View Mausoleum.

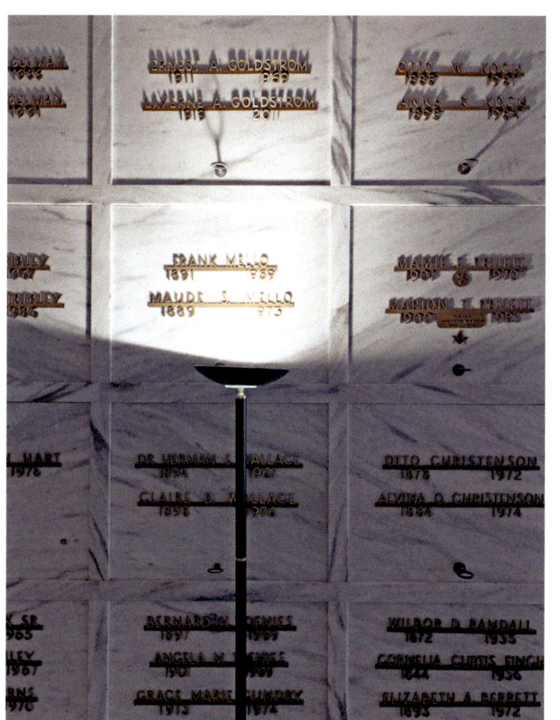

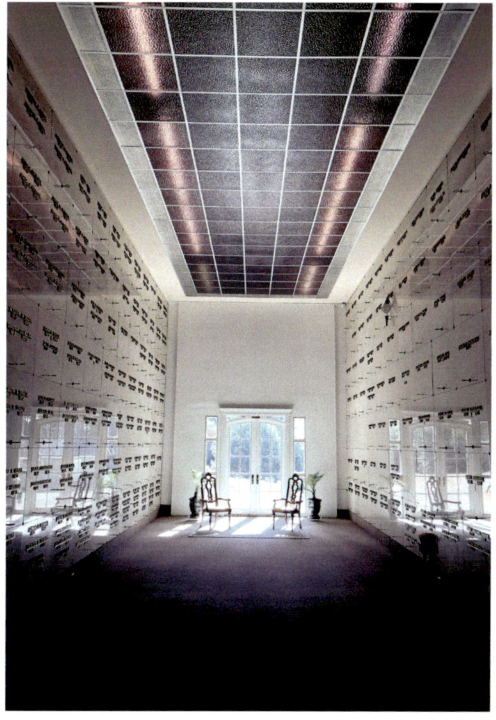

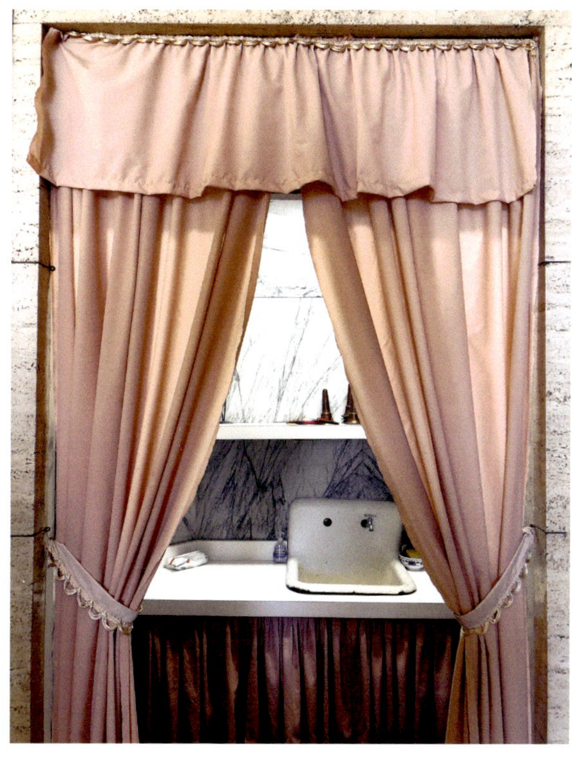

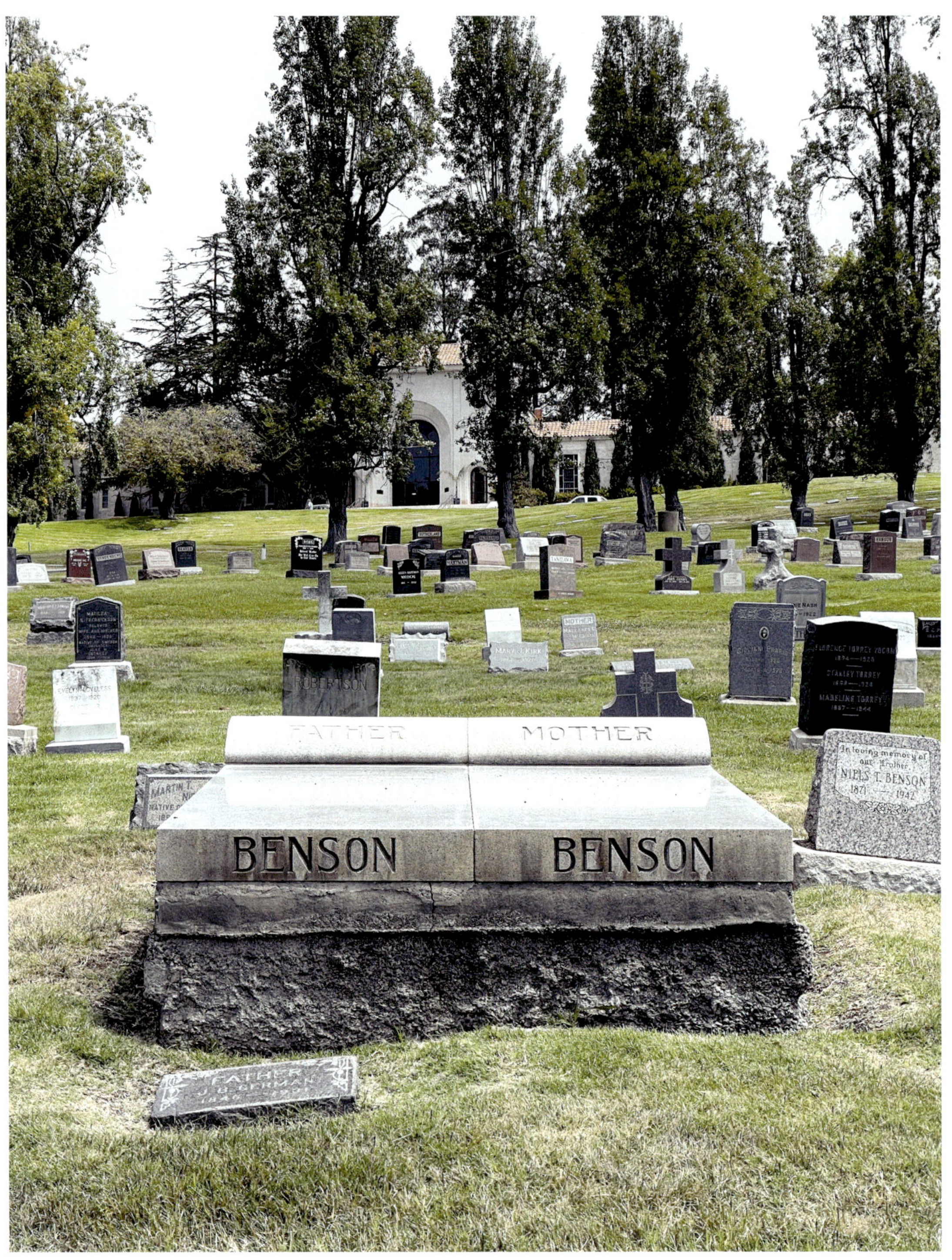

A bed crypt.

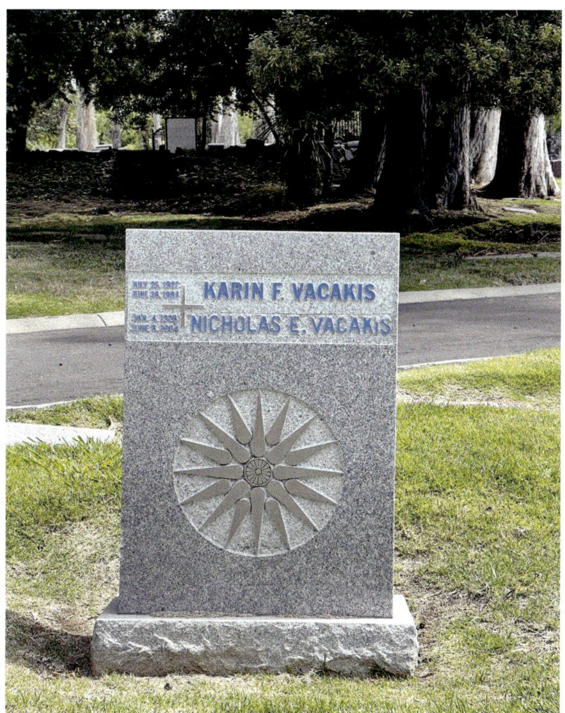

An interesting marker.

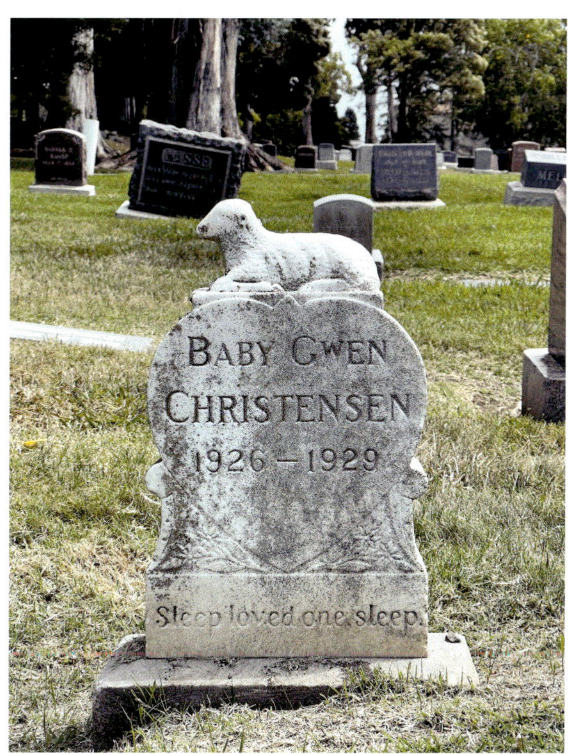

Sleep loved one sleep.

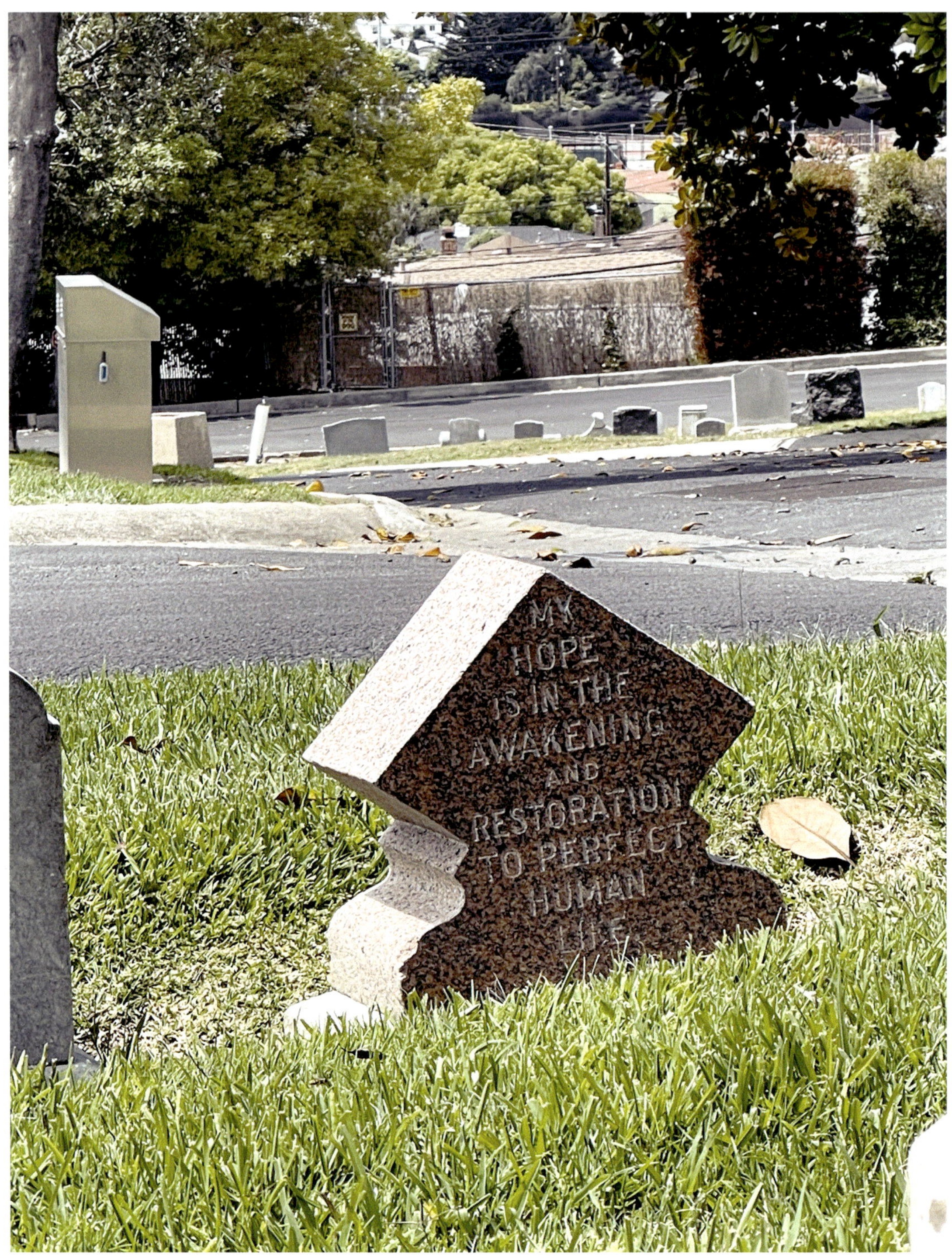

MY
HOPE
IS IN THE
AWAKENING
AND
RESTORATION
TO PERFECT
HUMAN
LIFE

My hope.

# 5

# COLMA

Colma is America's only necropolis, meaning a planned city of the dead. The town's motto is "it's good to be alive in Colma," where the dead outnumber the living 1,000 to 1.

Colma's seventeen (one is now a golf course, which seems to be theme in the U.S.) cemeteries reflect the communities of people and immigrants that make up the Bay Area: the pioneers at Cypress Lawn, Olivet, and Holy Cross, the Japanese and Chinese immigrants in their respective burial grounds, the Jewish refugees and immigrants across a span of time that measures three cemeteries in Colma, the Italian cemetery, the Serbian cemetery, the Greek Orthodox Cemetery, and yes, even the Pet Cemetery, for pets of the children of the cemetery workers.

The atmosphere in Colma is, frankly, surreal. As one drives up and over a small hill after exiting the highway, the stretch of El Camino Real is visible far down the road, with thousands upon thousands of headstones on either side, behind several car dealerships and a large Home Depot. It's as if 100 years of history was simply picked up and placed here. But of course, that's what happened.

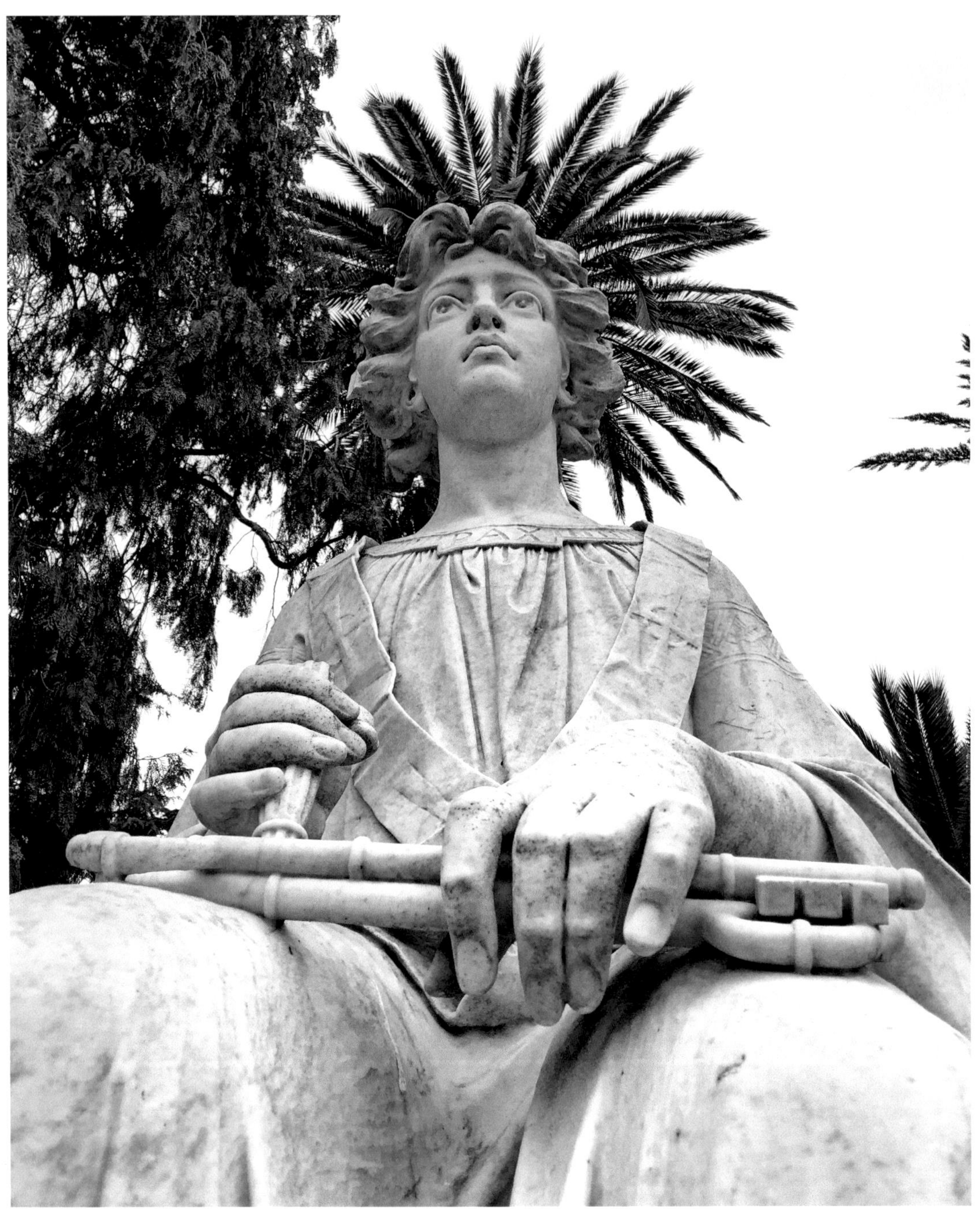

The Angel Gabriel at Cypress Lawn.

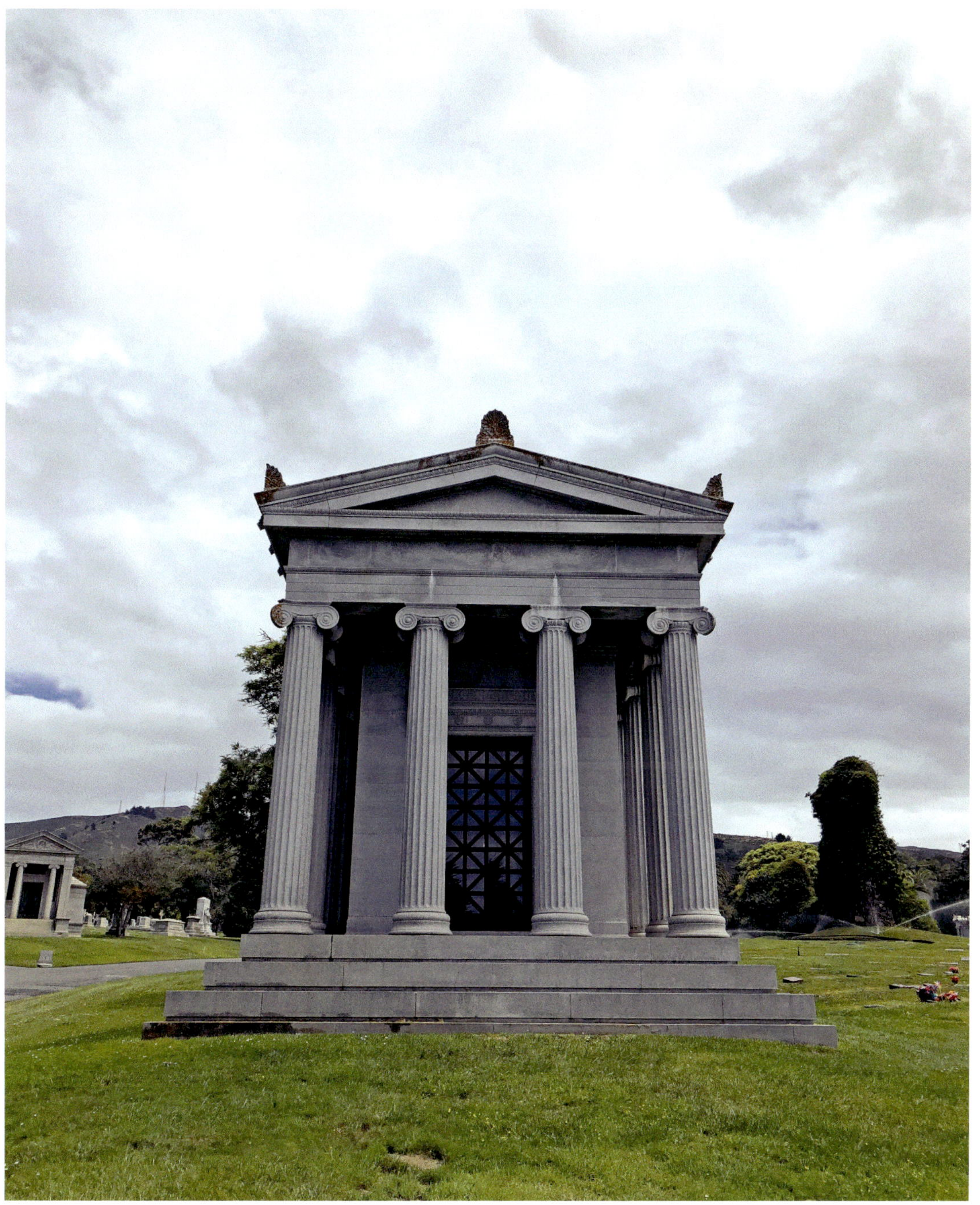

The Hearst mausoleum at Cypress Lawn, burial place of William Randolph Hearst.

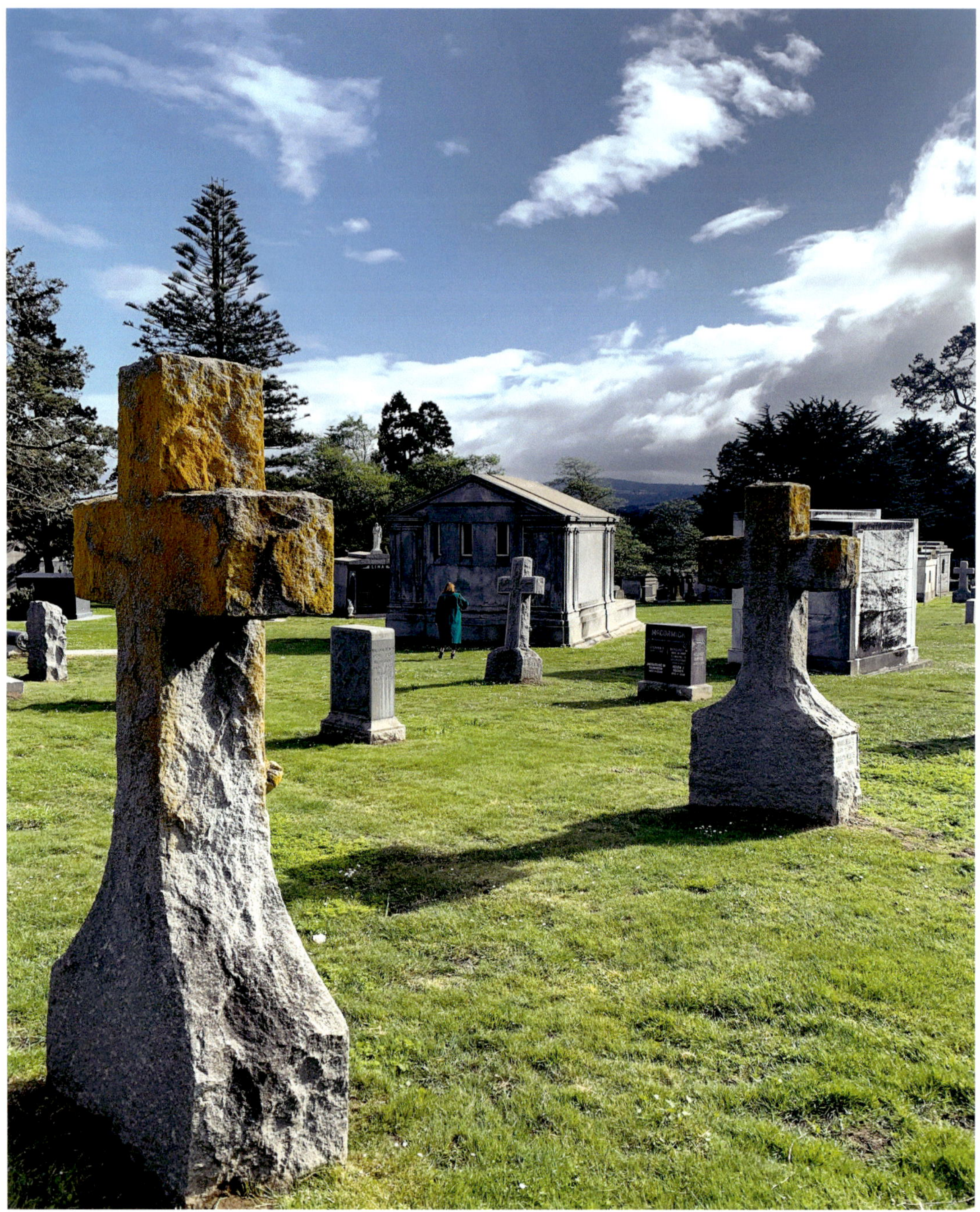

Among the tombstones at Holy Cross.

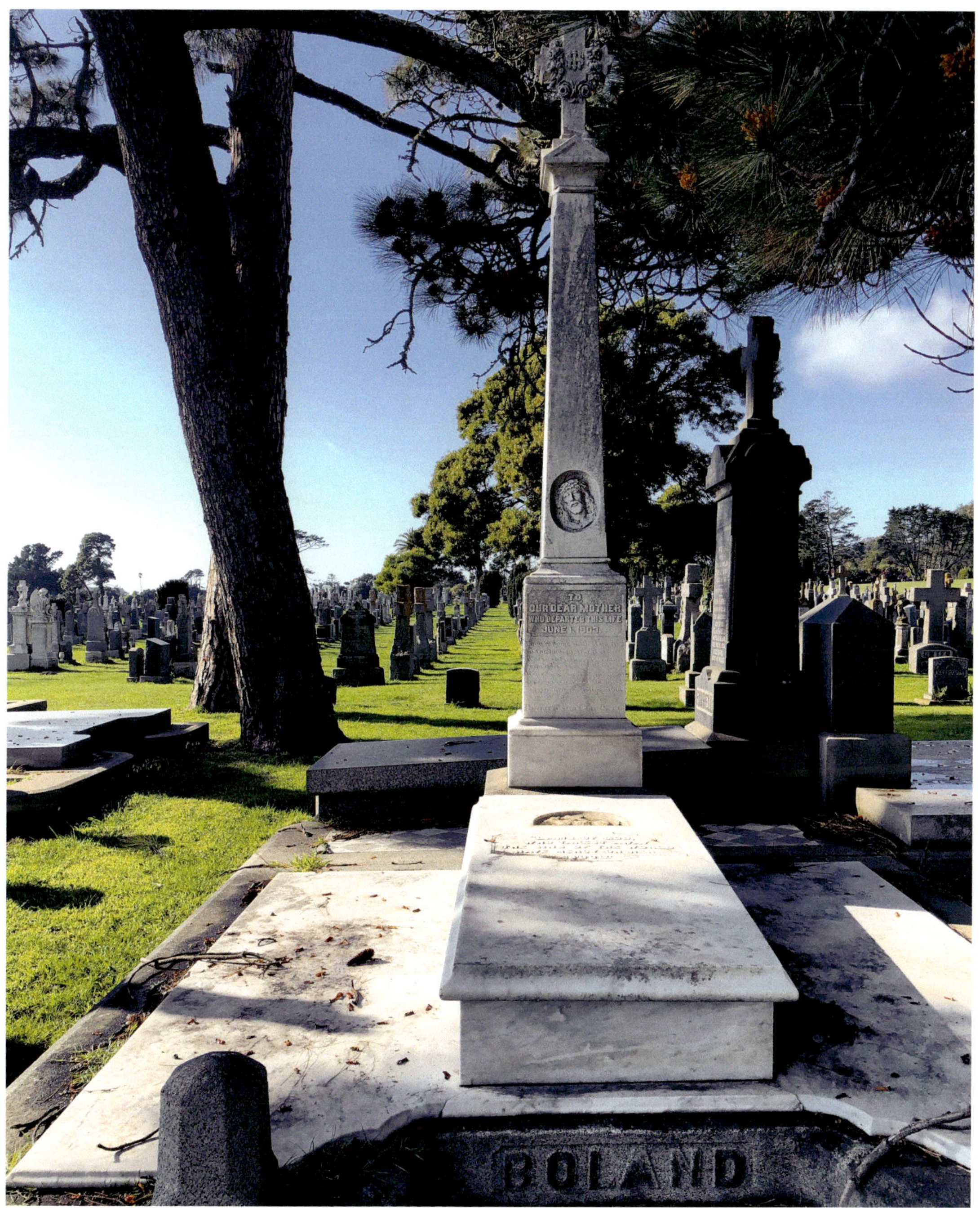

Catholic iconography, the suffering Christ.

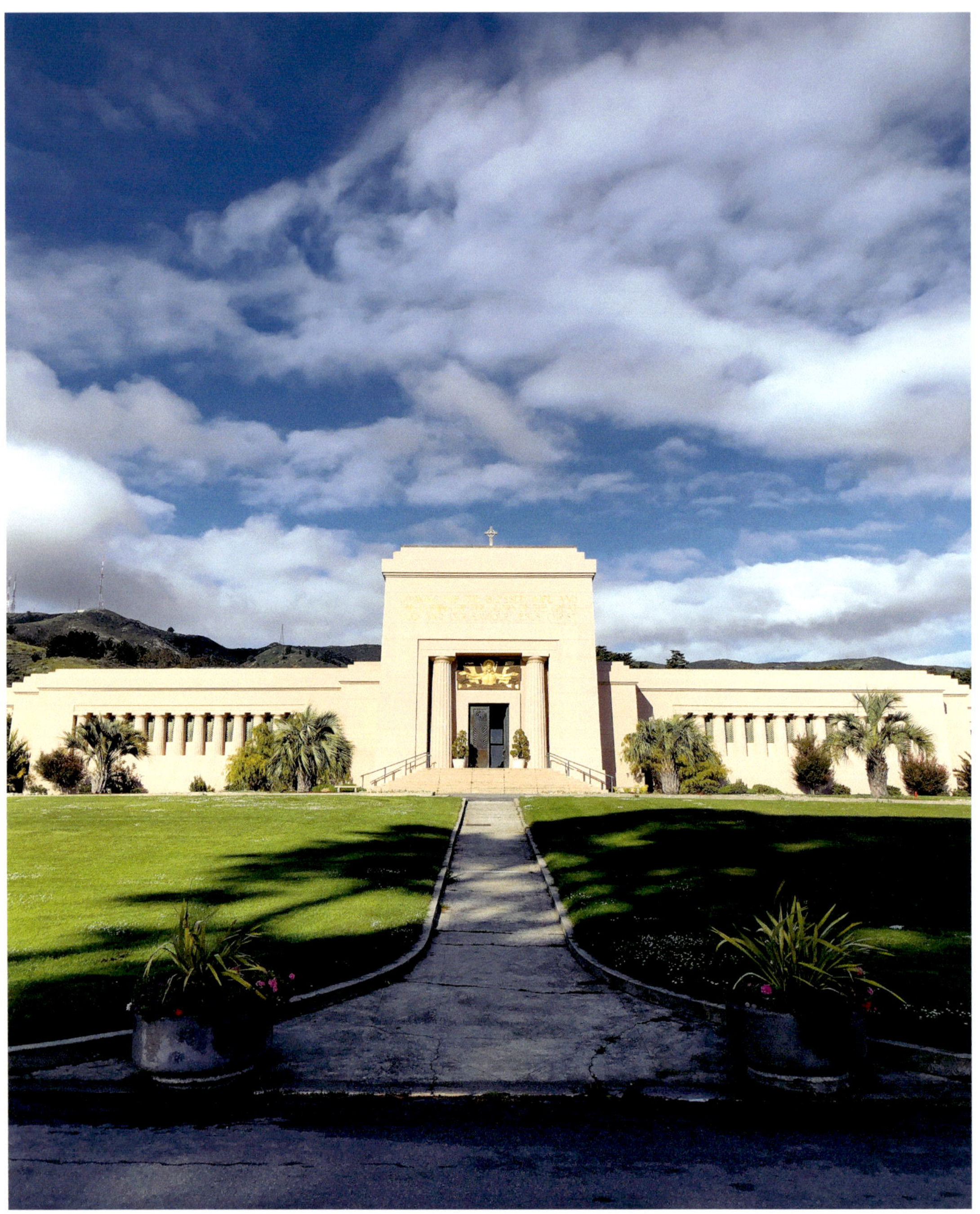

The Mausoleum at Holy Cross.

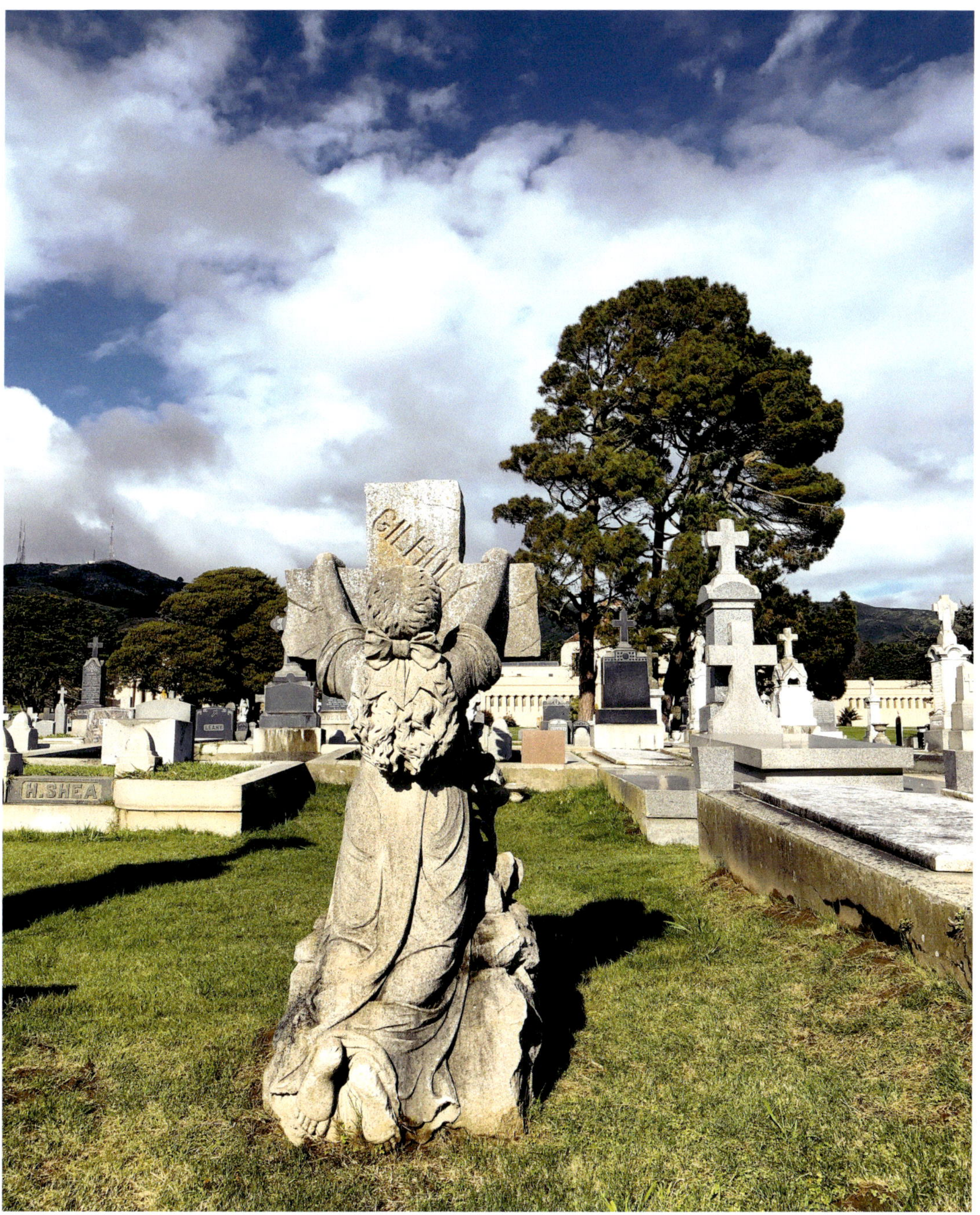

Clinging to the cross.

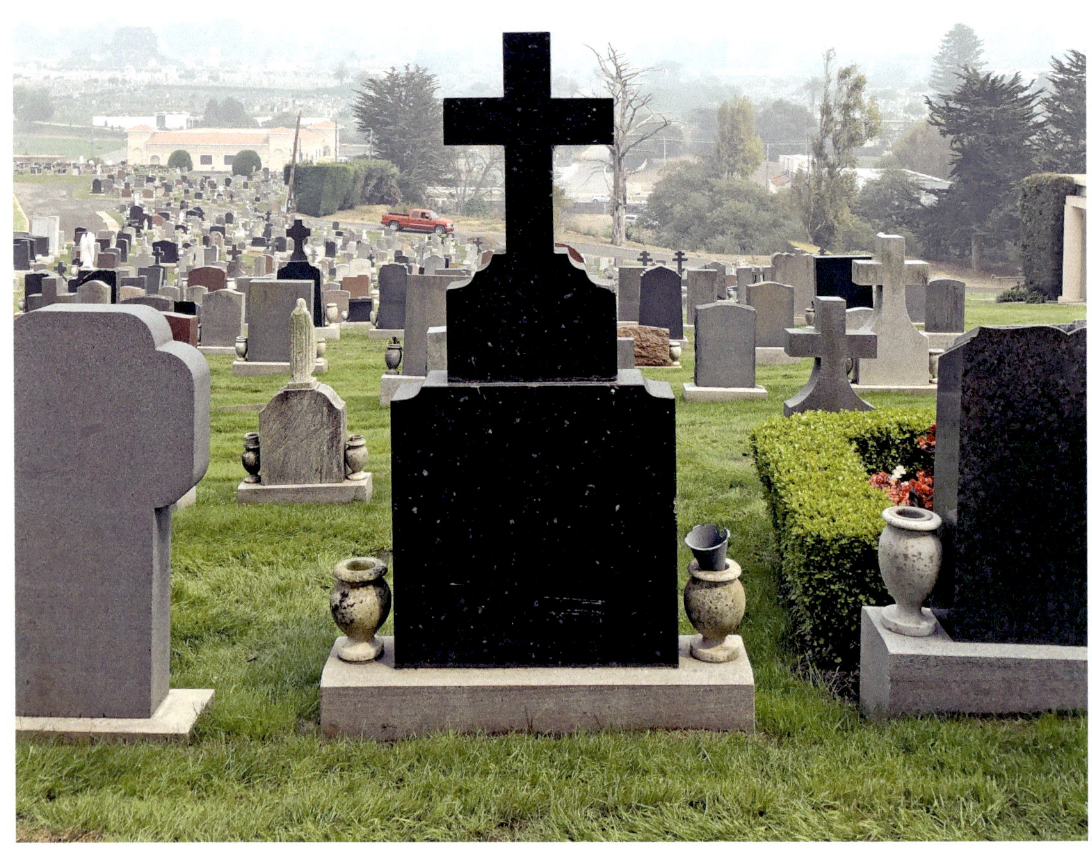

The Greek Orthodox Cemetery.

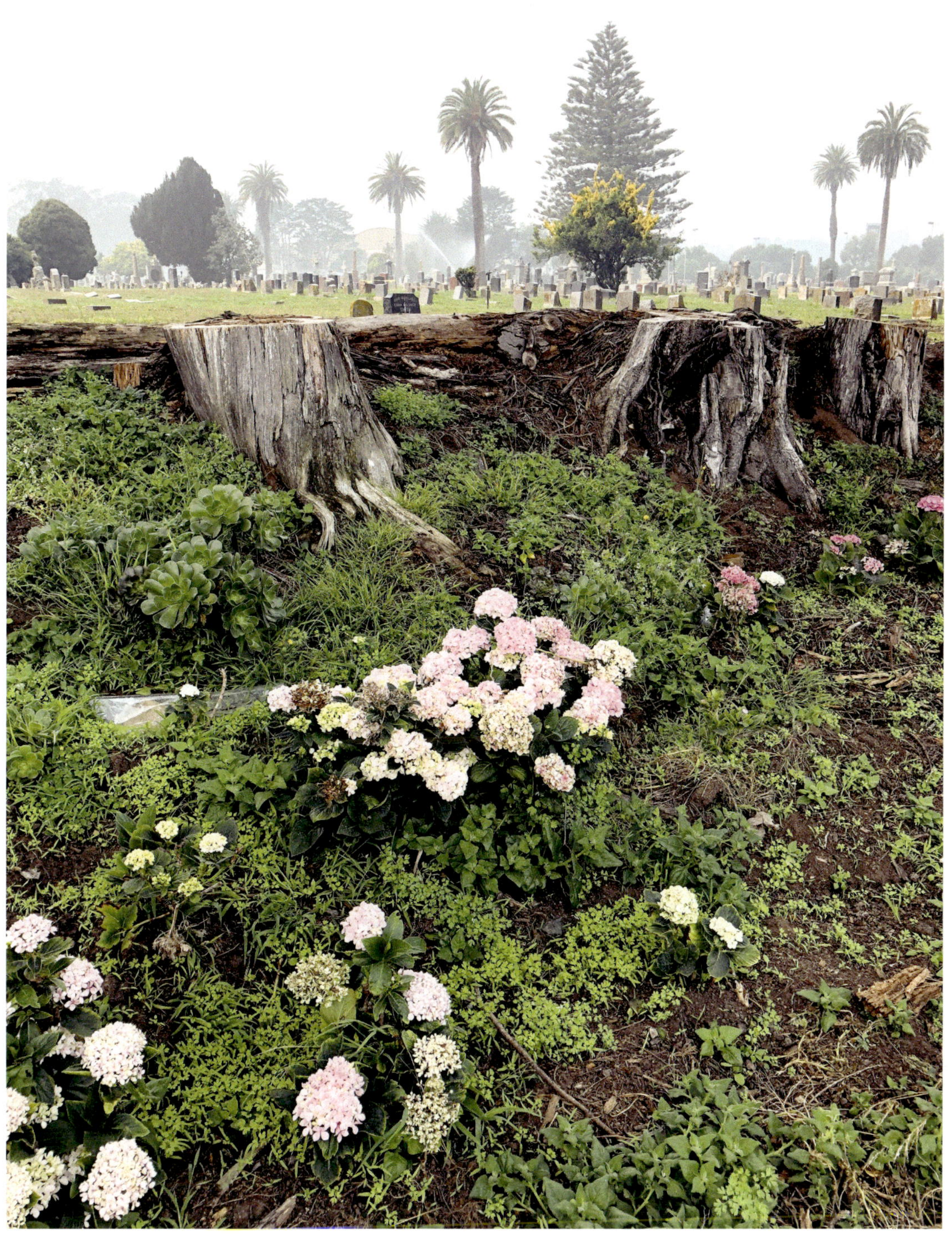

The line between Greek Orthodox and Greenlawn Cemetery.

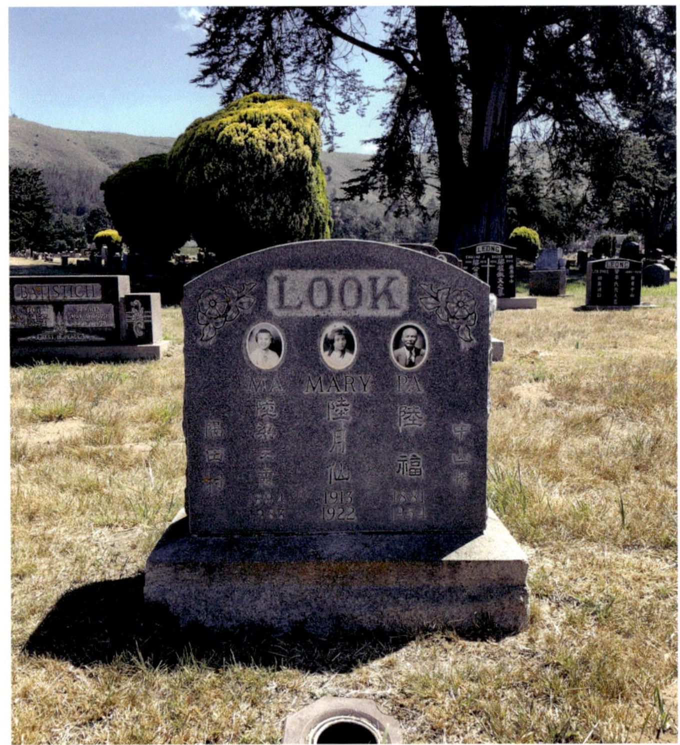

The Look Family at Mt. Olivet.

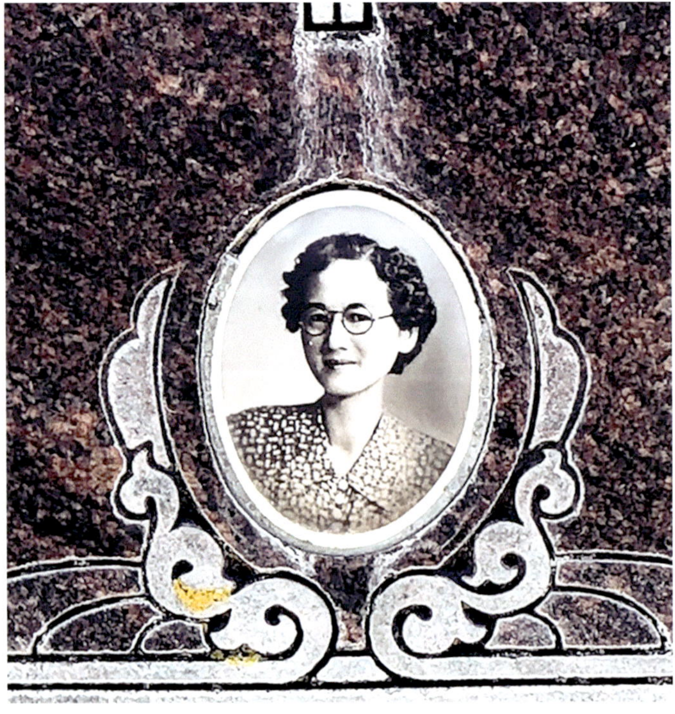

A permanent resident of Mt. Olivet.

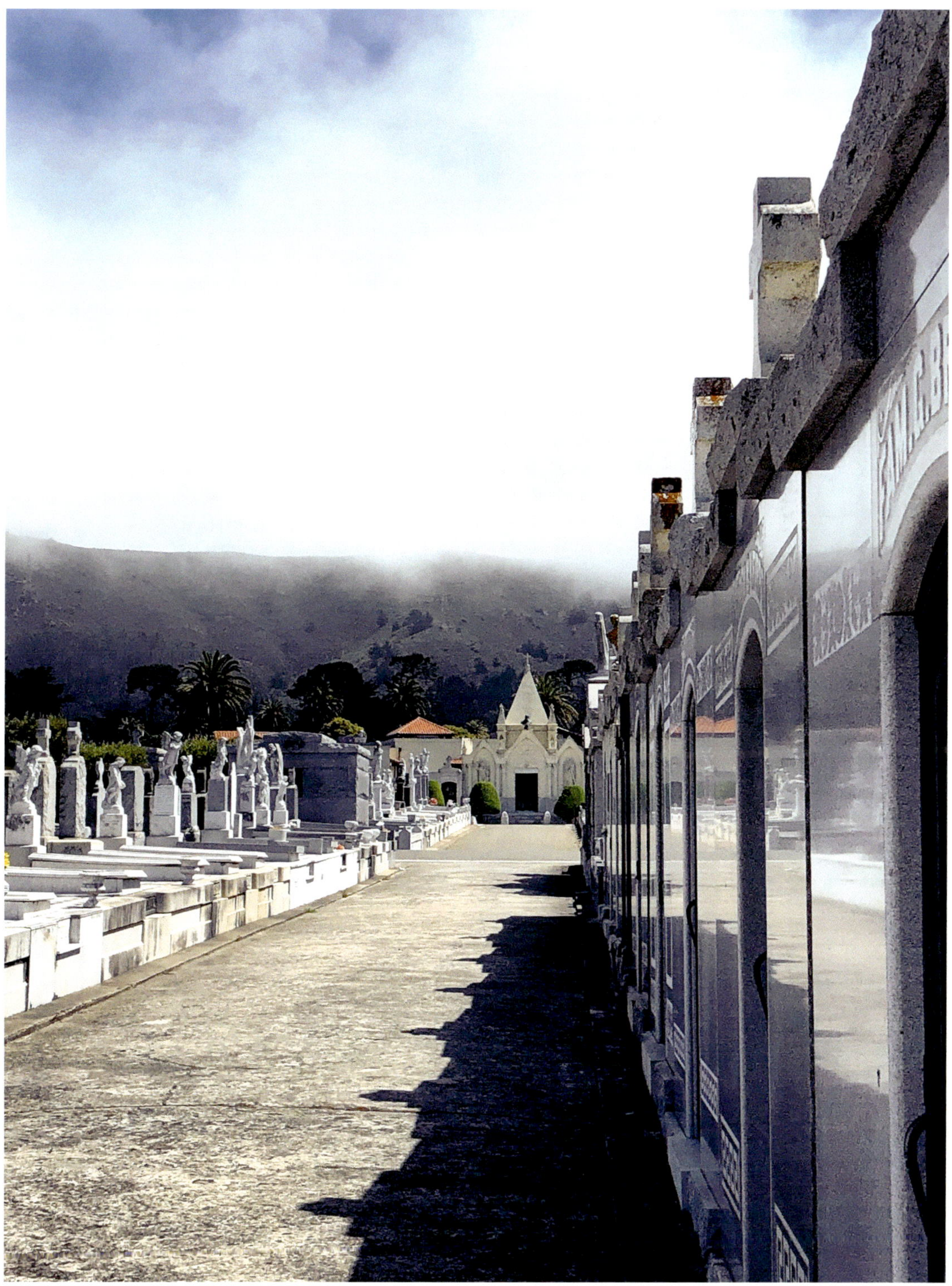

The unbelievably beautiful Italian Cemetery at Colma.

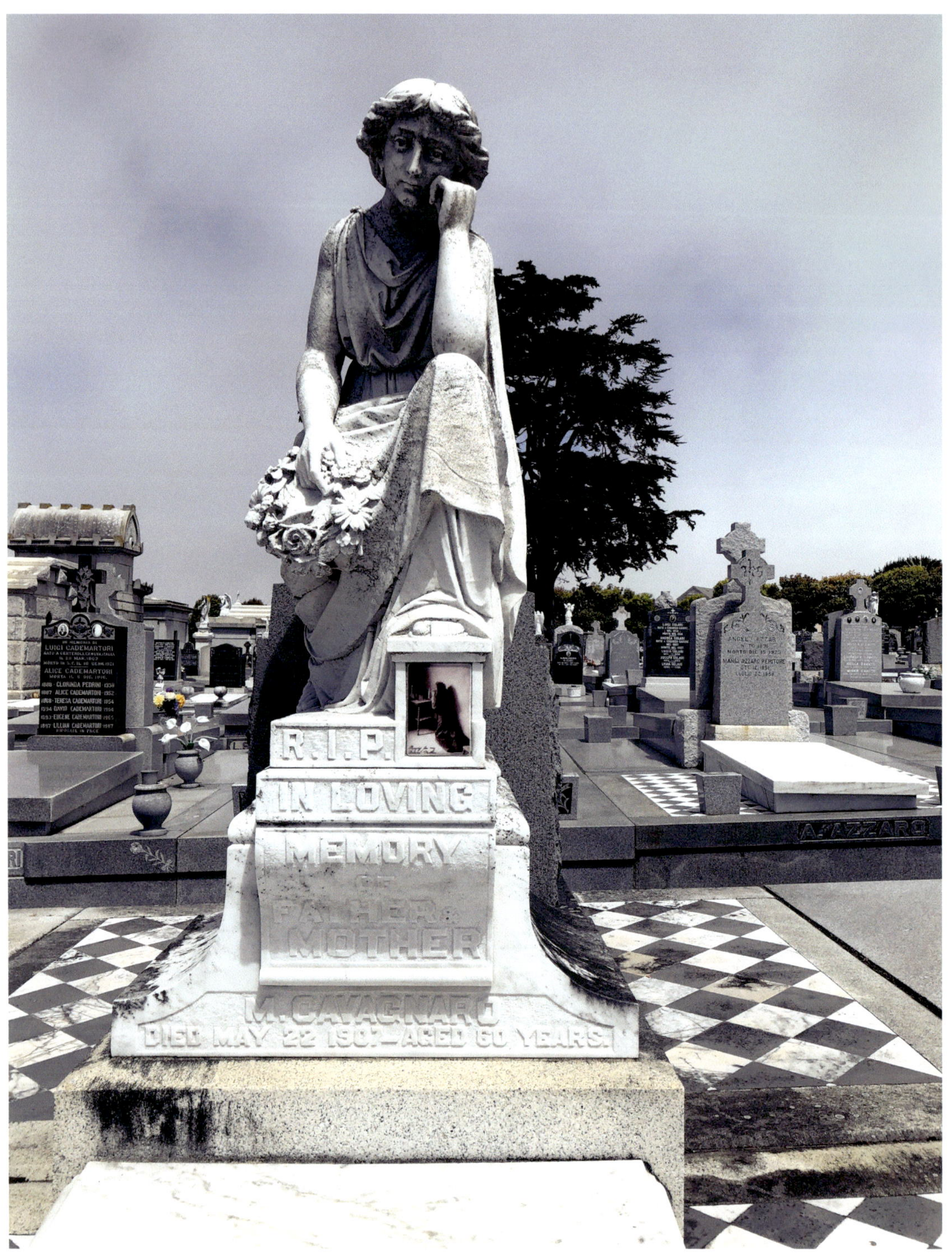


An angel perches in memory.

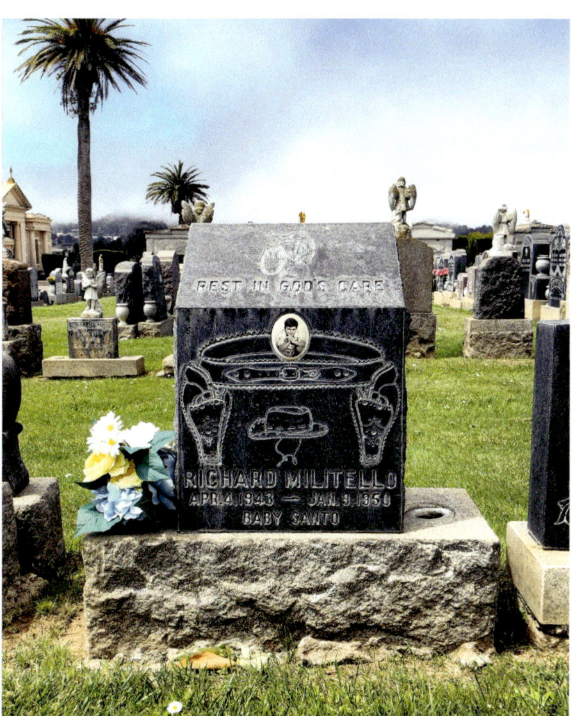


Sainted baby, a boy who drowned rescuing a friend.

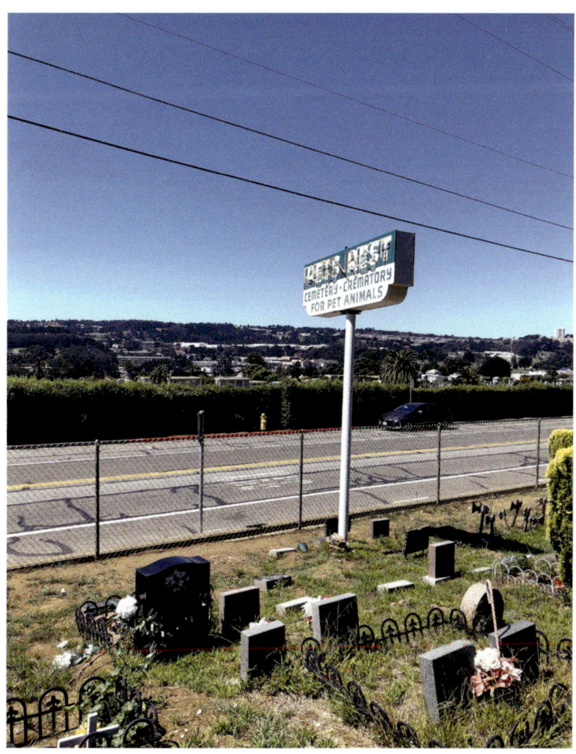


Pets Rest Cemetery in Colma.

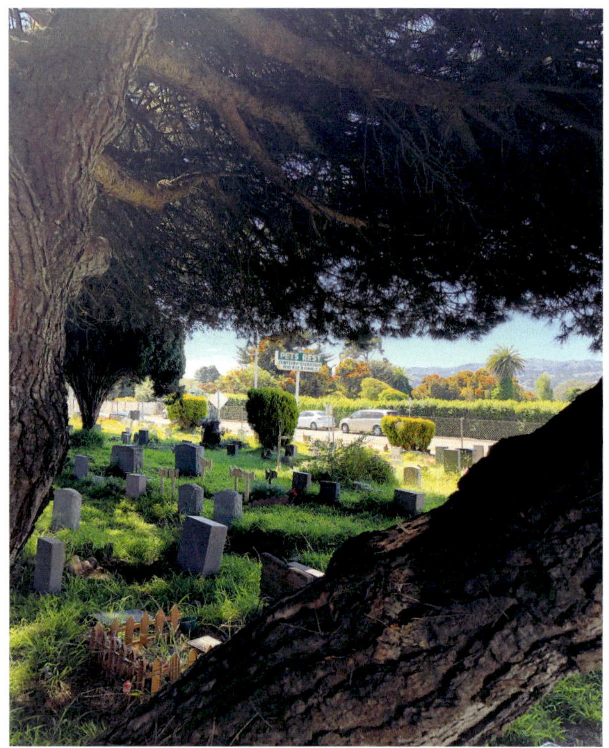

Pets Rest was established to accommodate the employees of Cypress Lawn's children, whose pets needed a place to rest.

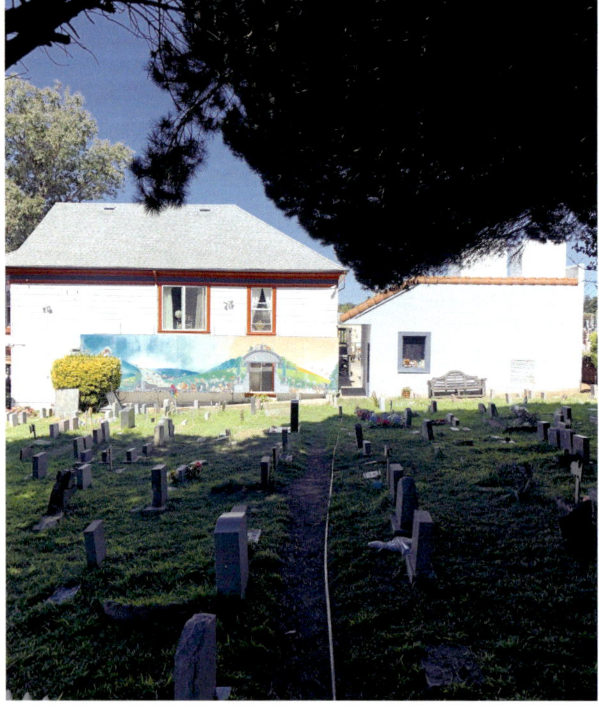

The cemetery is still very much an active cemetery and mortuary.

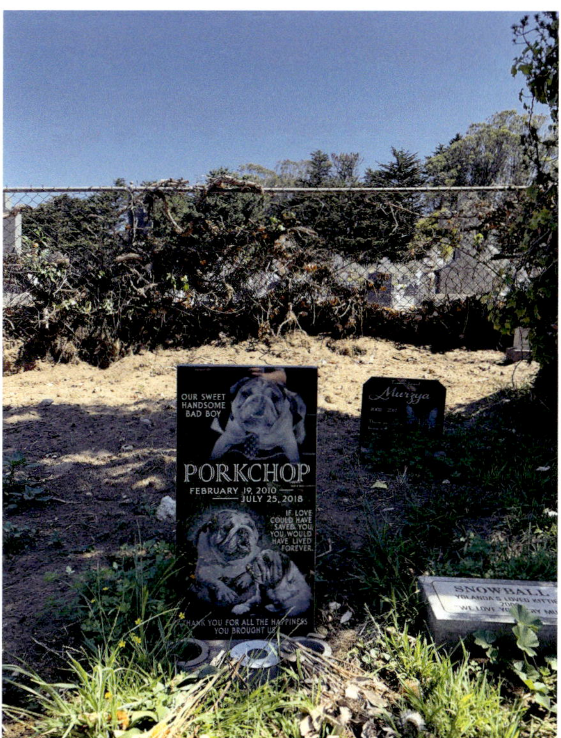

Our sweet, handsome boy.

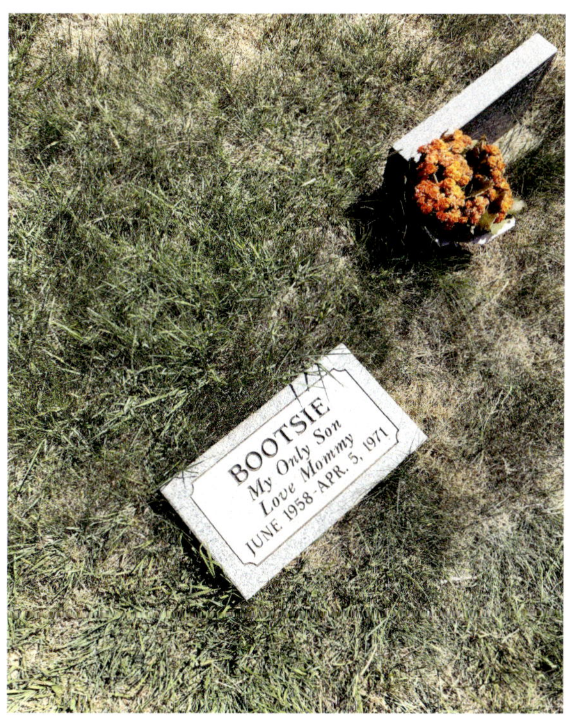

My only son.

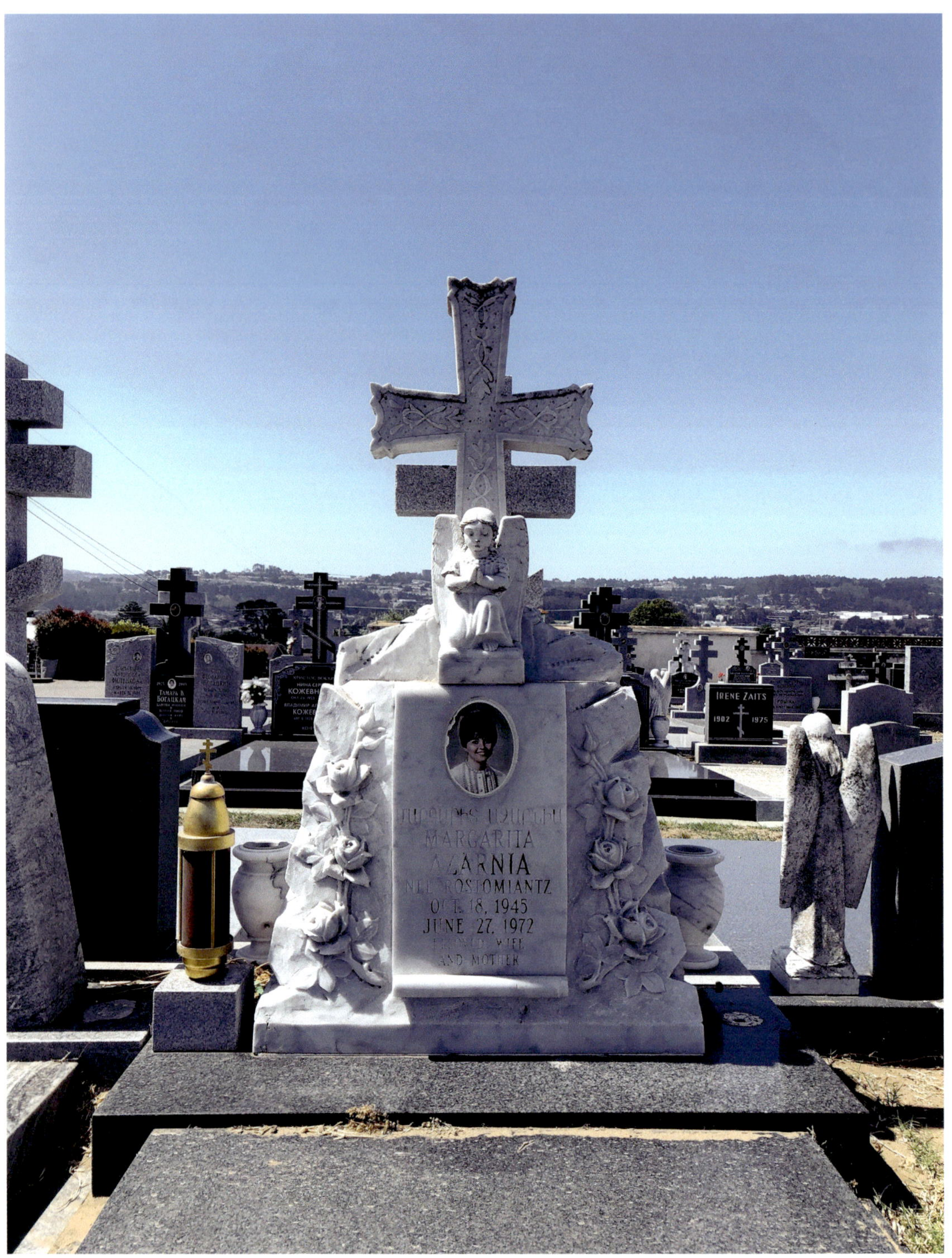


A young mother at the Serbian Cemetery.

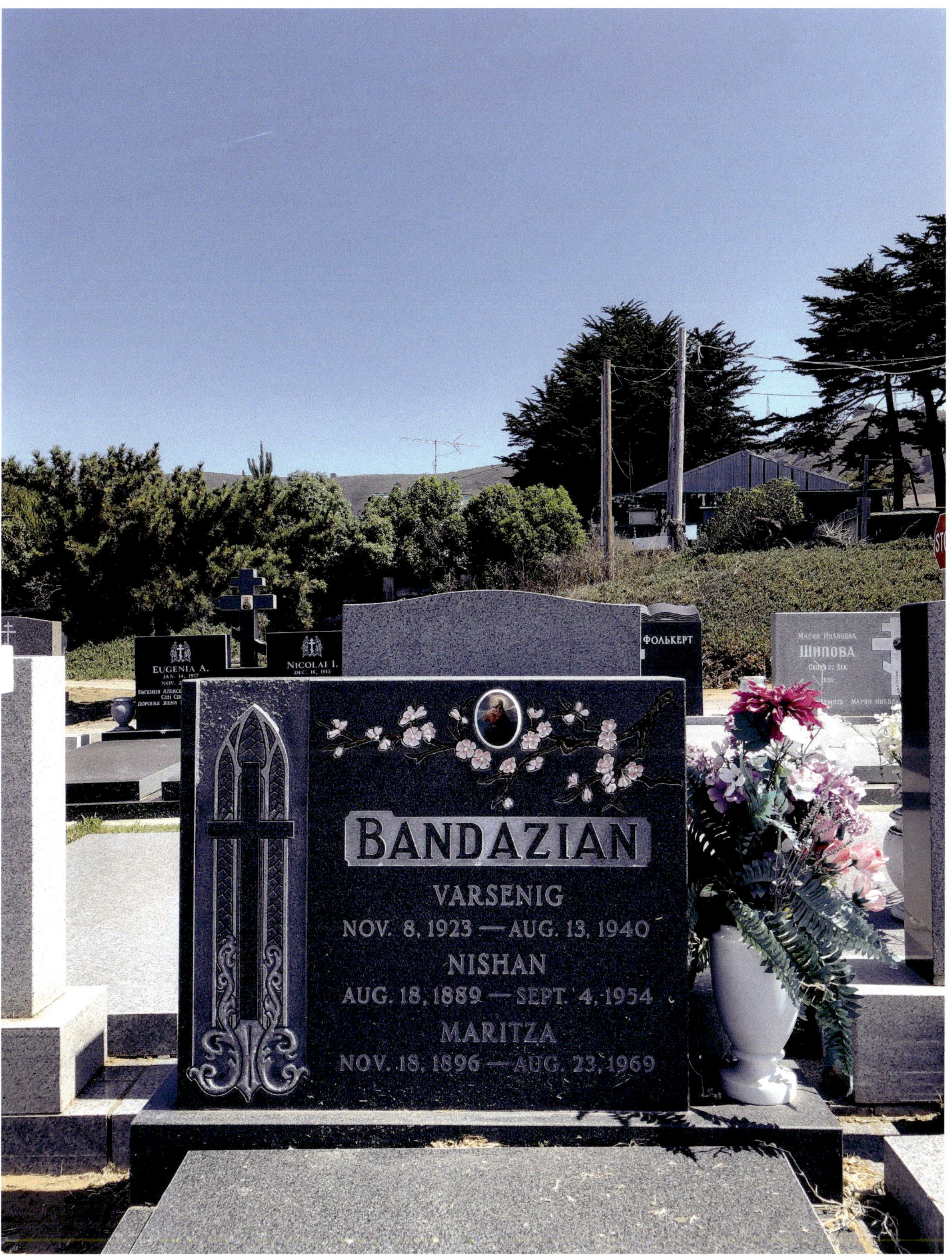



An Armenian family plot.

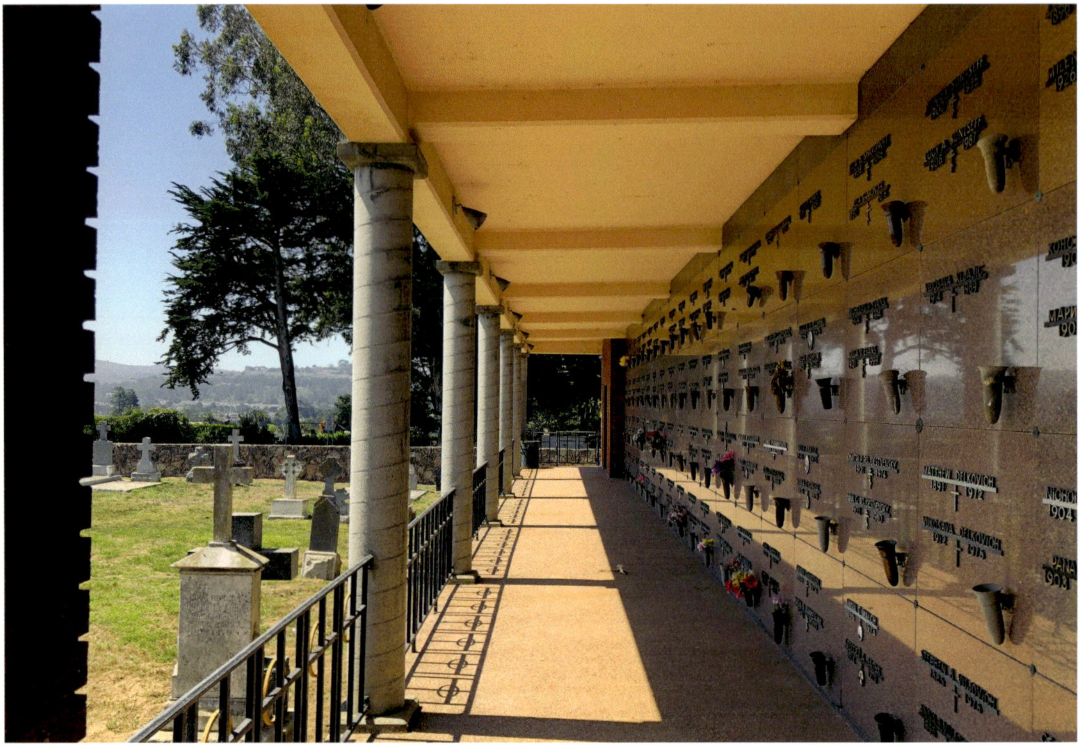

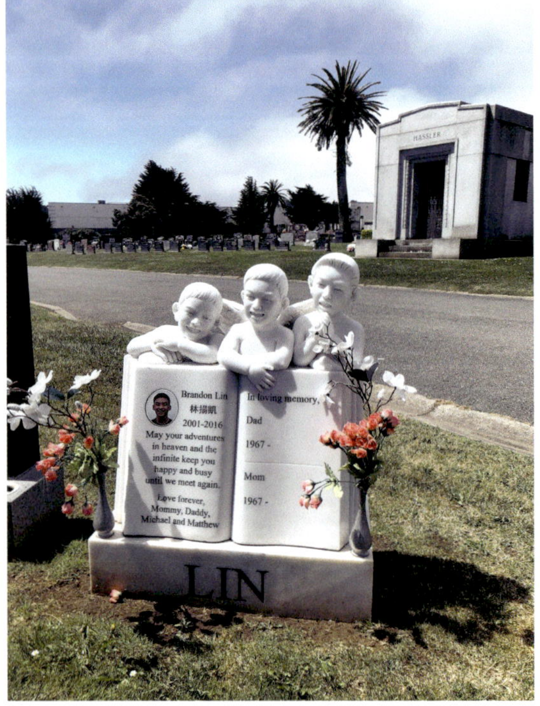

*Above:* A view of the Serbian Cemetery from the wall crypt.

*Left:* Two brothers with their angel brother at Woodlawn Cemetery.

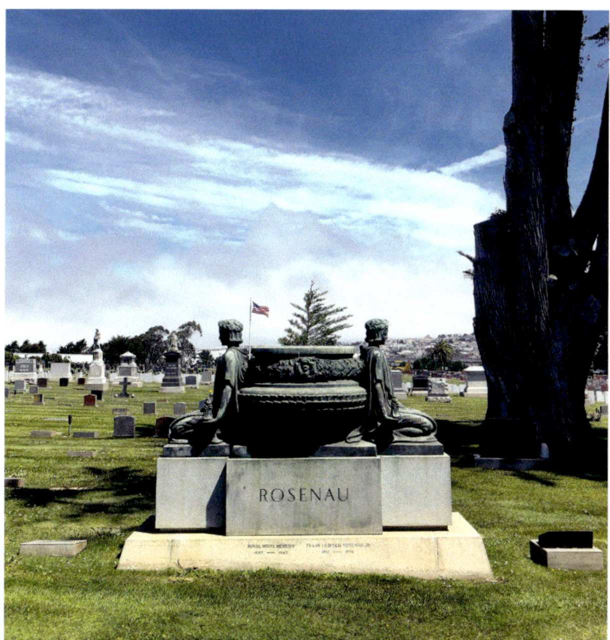

The Rosenau family memorial with the sun burning off the morning fog.

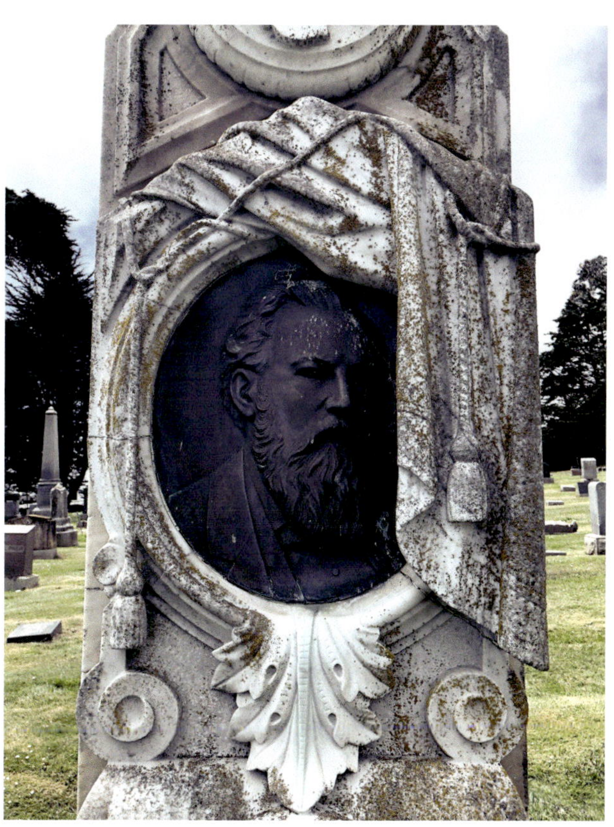

A bearded gentleman.

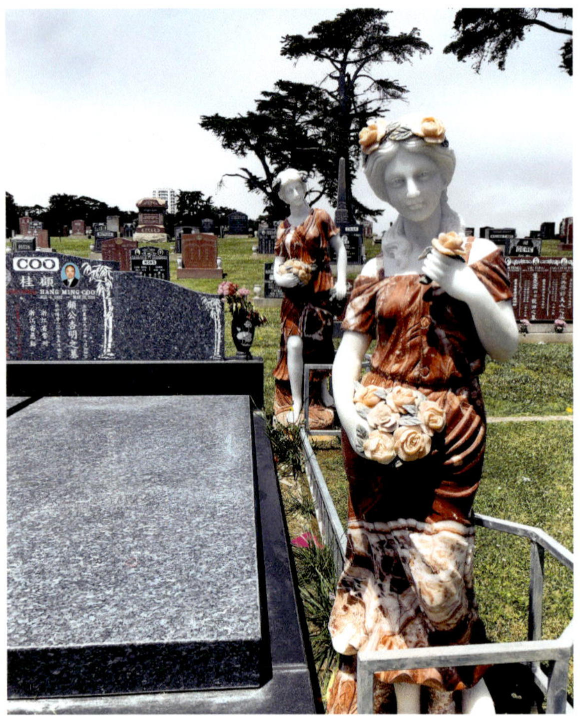

A Chinese memorial.

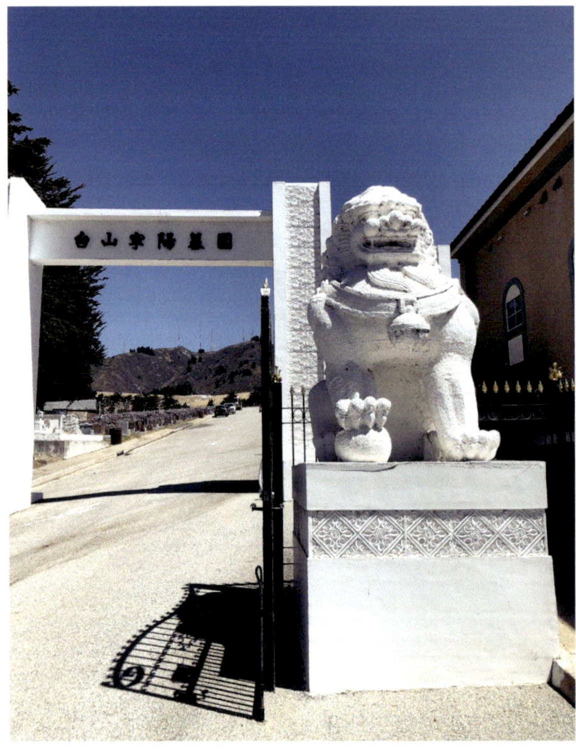



Foo dogs guard the entrance to Hoy Sun, a Chinese cemetery in Colma.

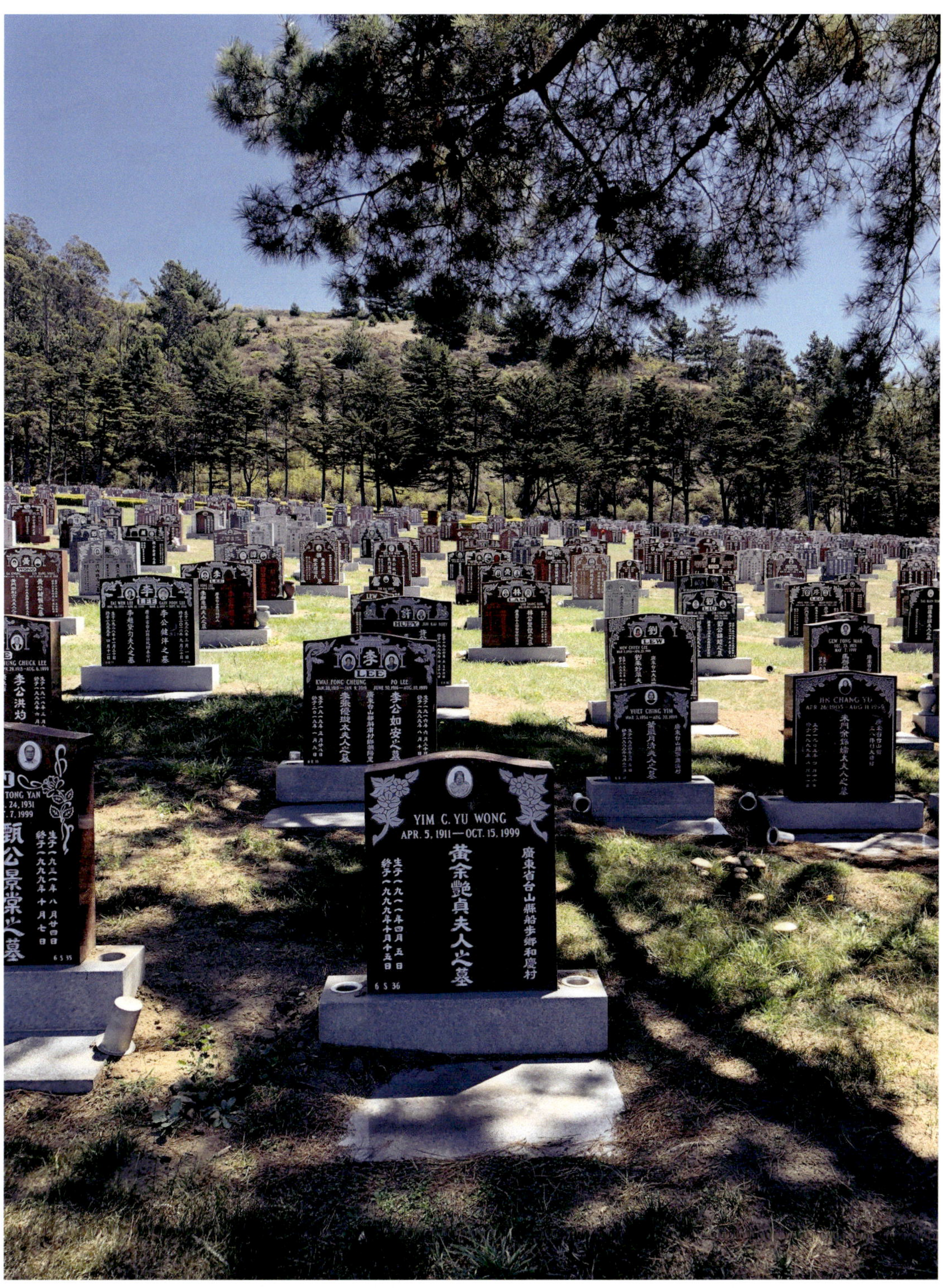

Chinese family graves at Hoy Sun.

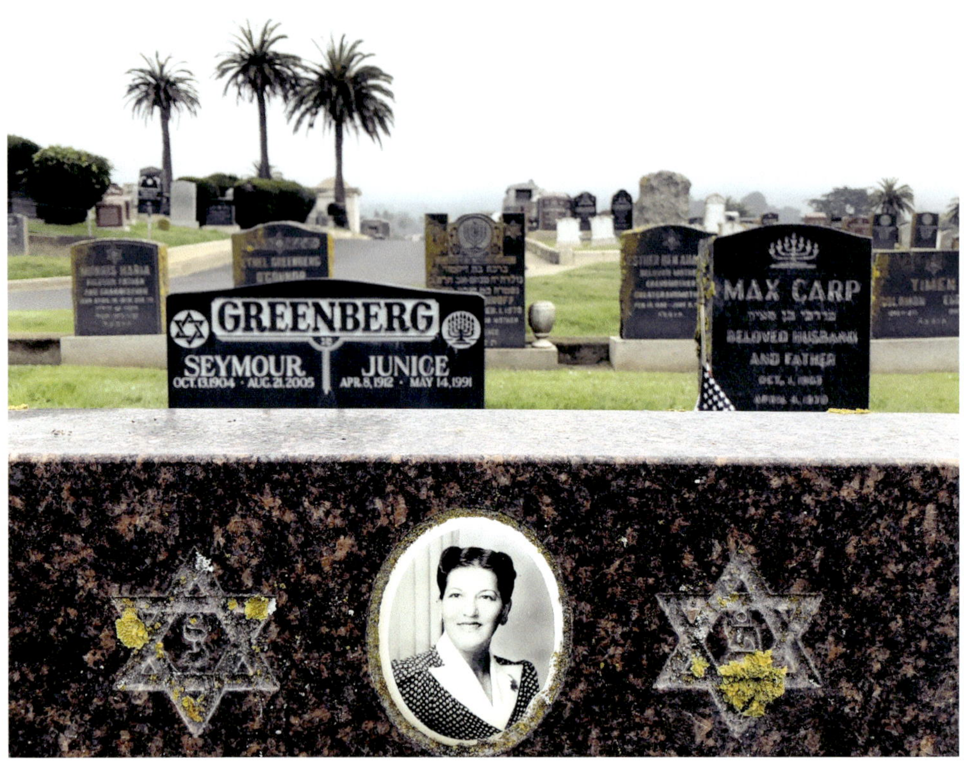

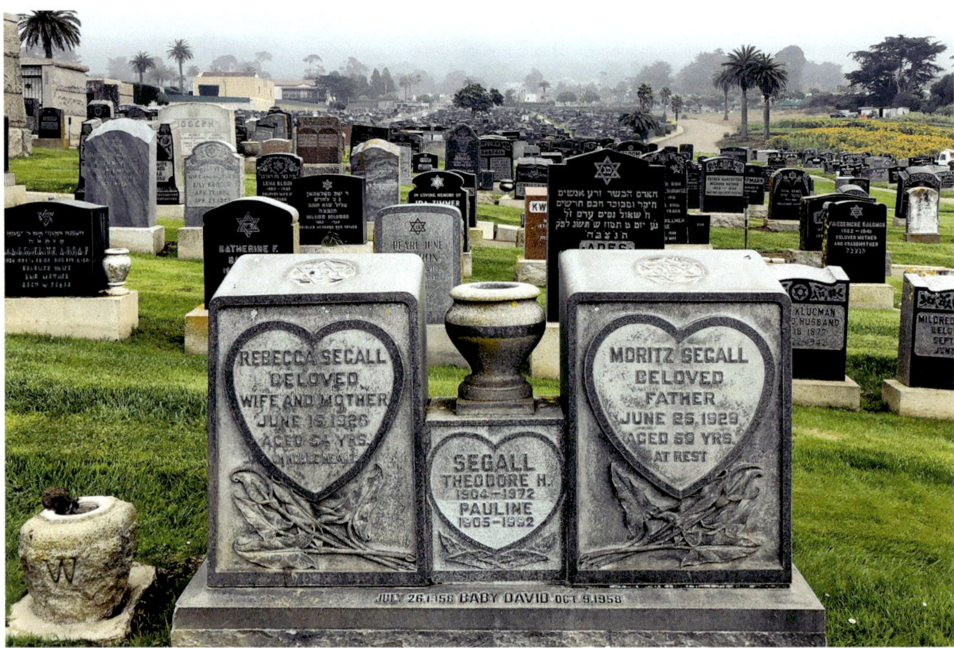

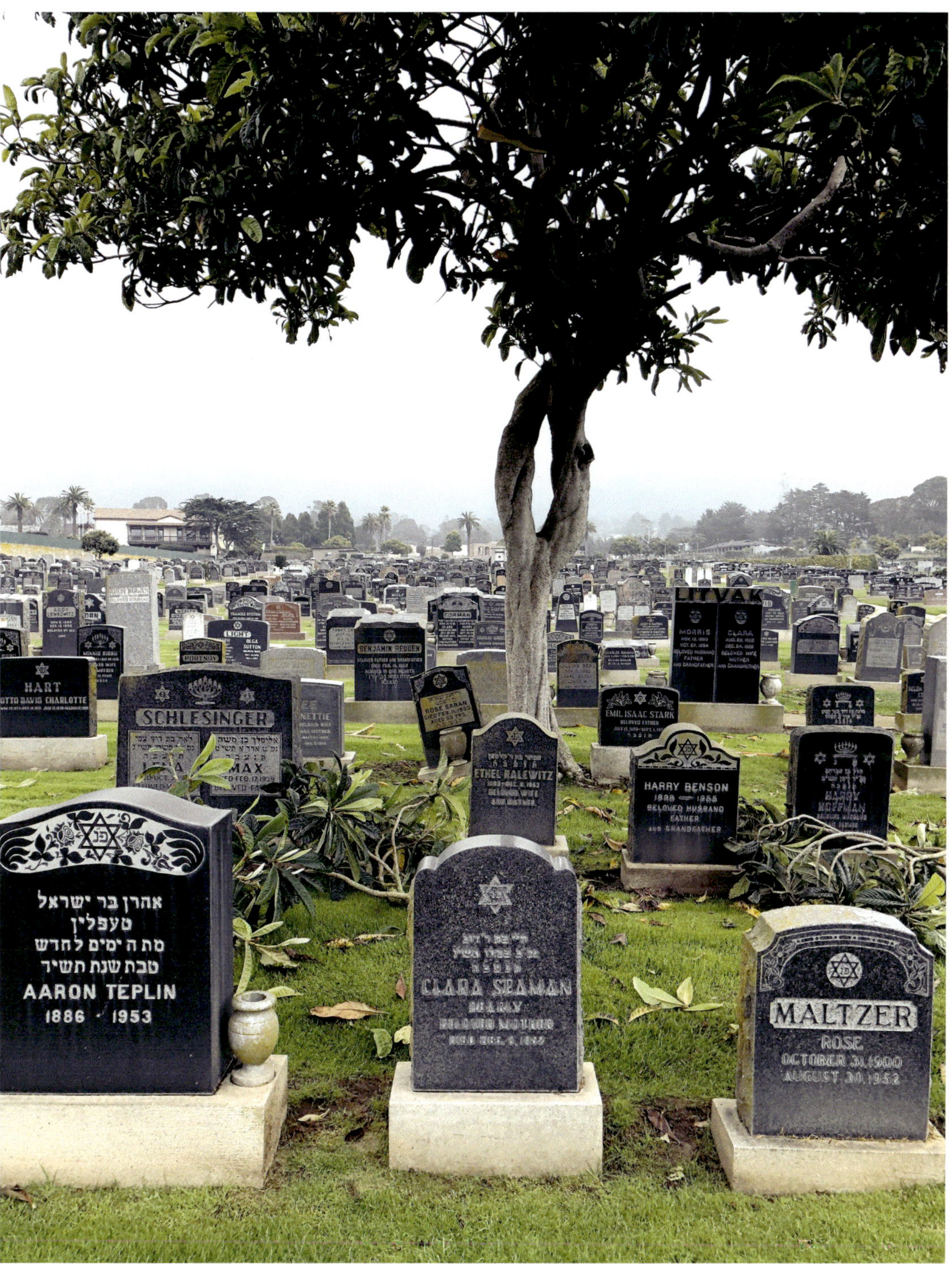

*These pages:*  Headstones at Eternal Home Jewish Cemetery in Colma.

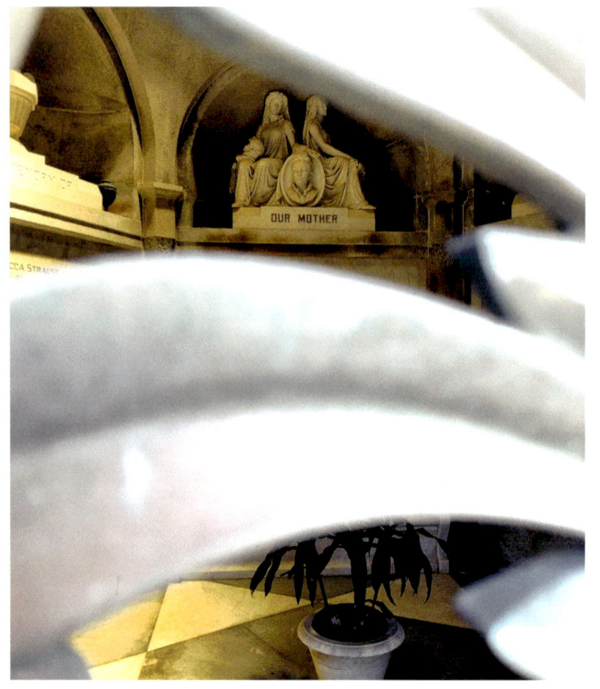

The Levi Strauss mausoleum, at Home of Peace Jewish Cemetery in Colma.

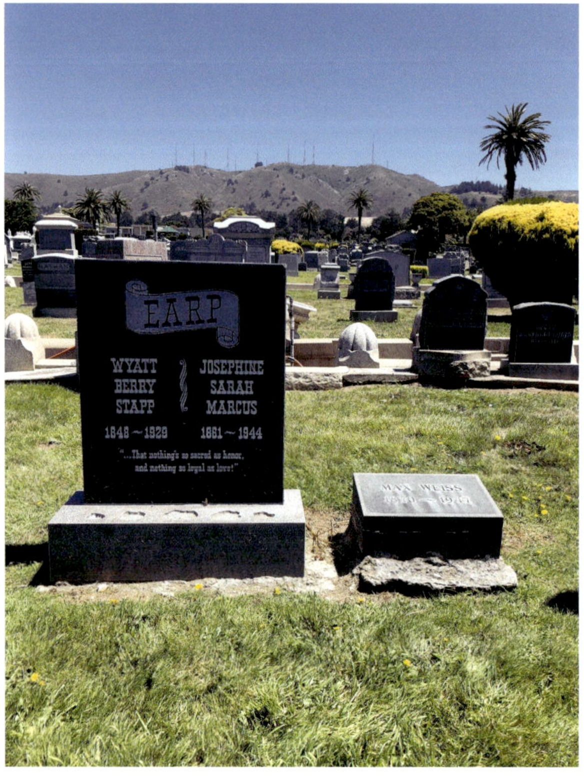

Wyatt Earp, whose wife was Jewish.

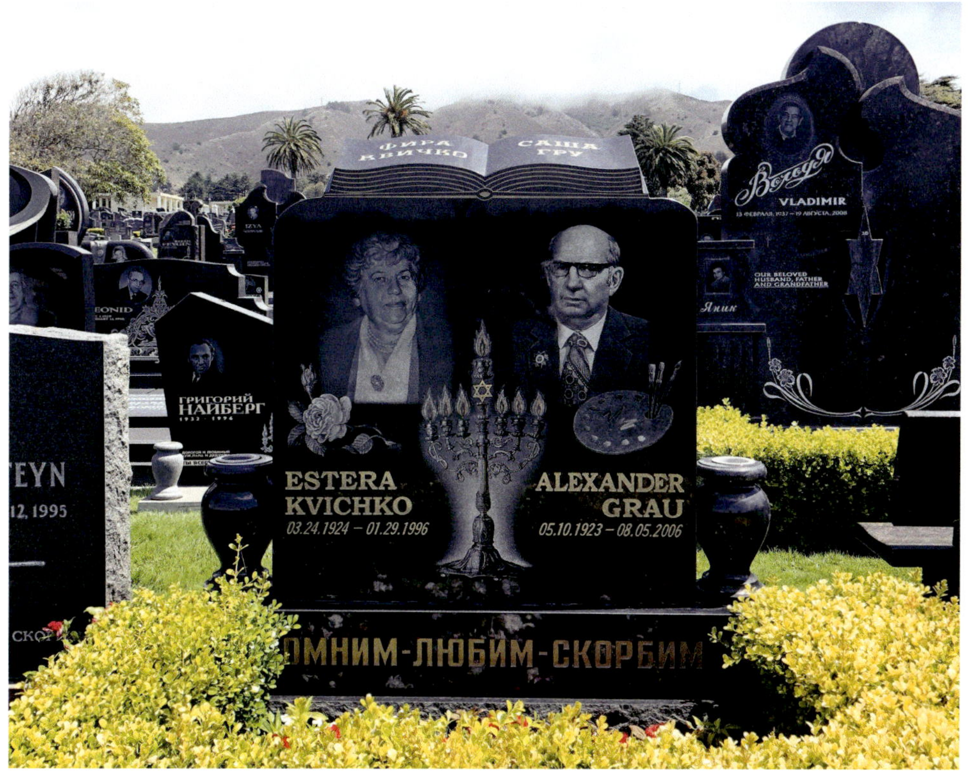



*Above and right:* Unbelievably artistic and ornate memorials at Home of Peace.

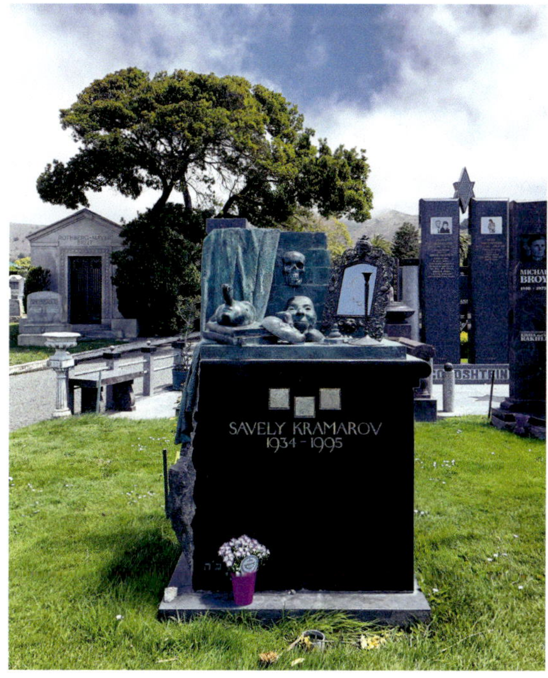

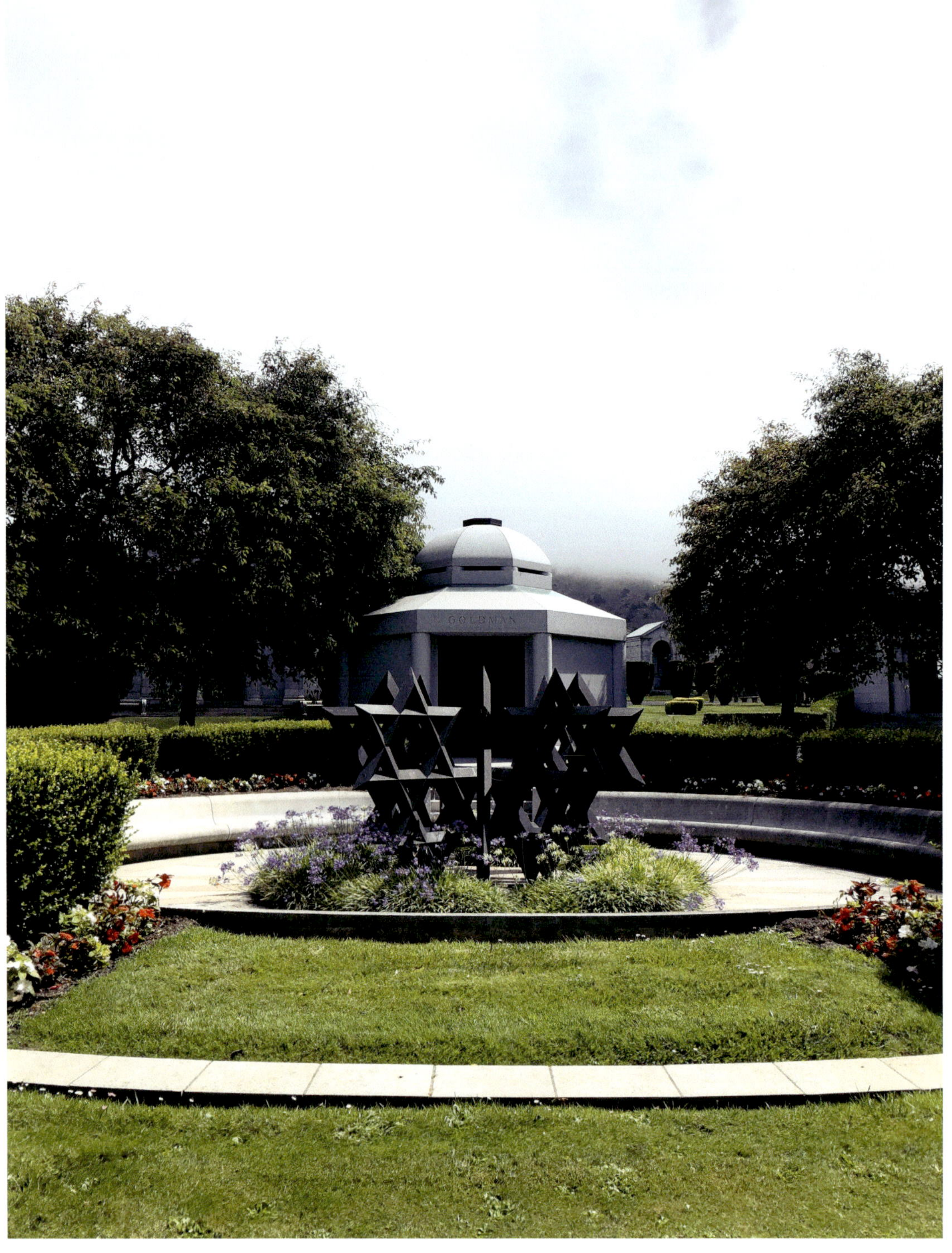

A mausoleum in front of a fountain with the Star of David.

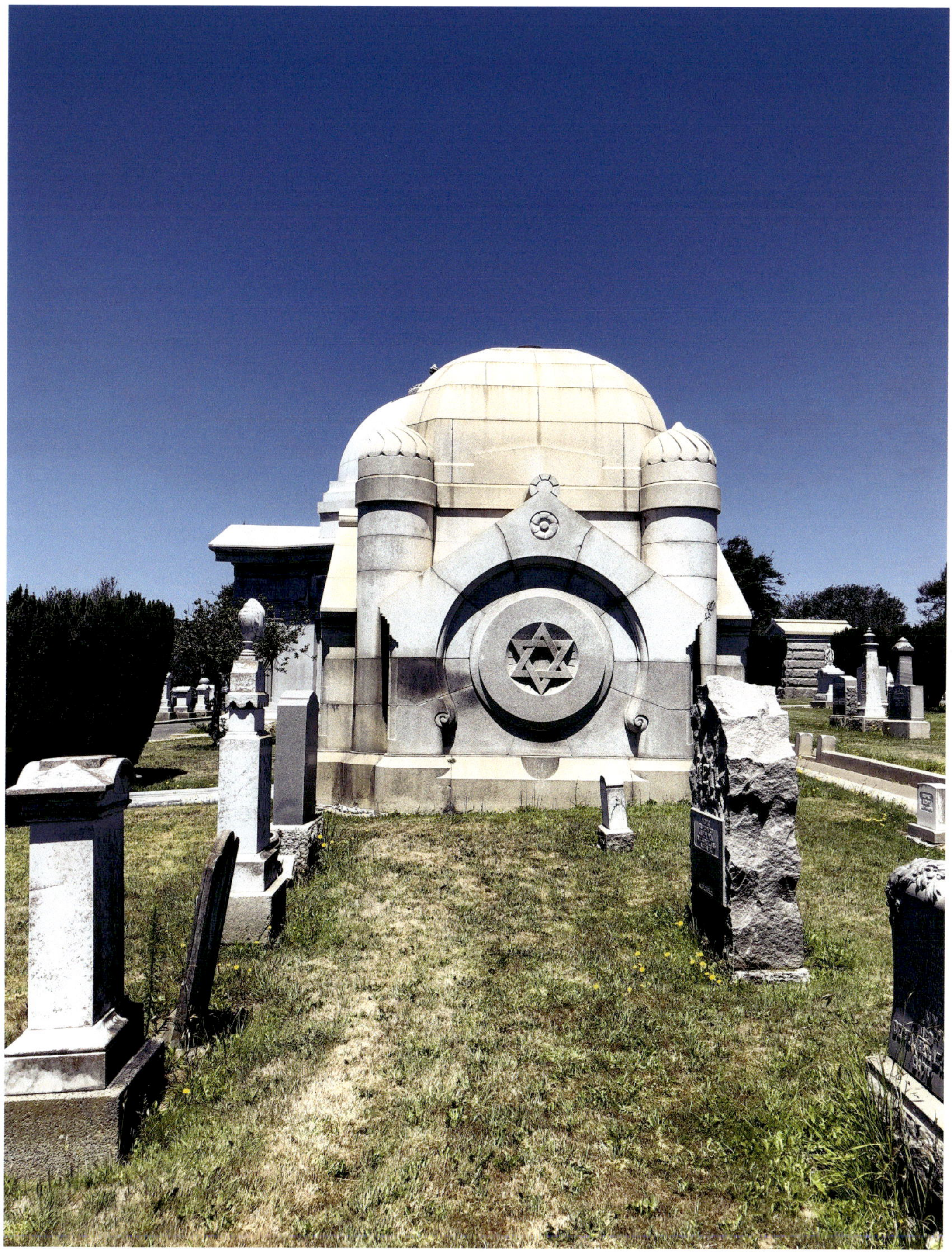

The Star of David adorns the side of the Levi-Strauss mausoleum.

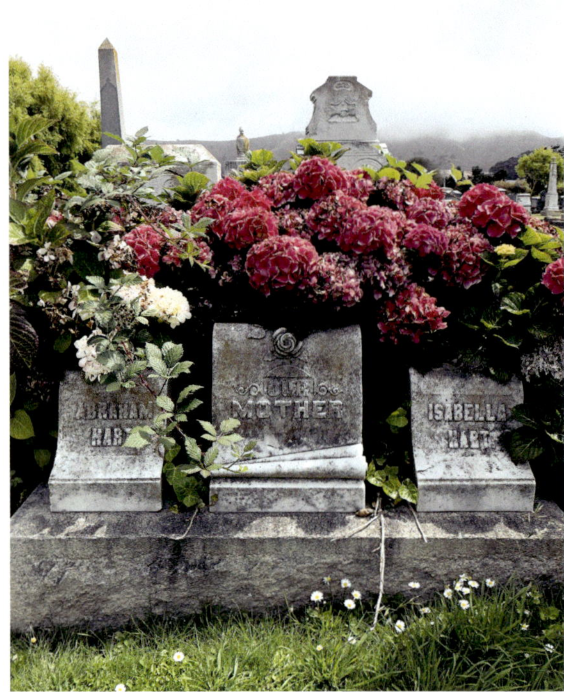

Breathtaking hydrangeas at Salem Jewish Cemetery in Colma.

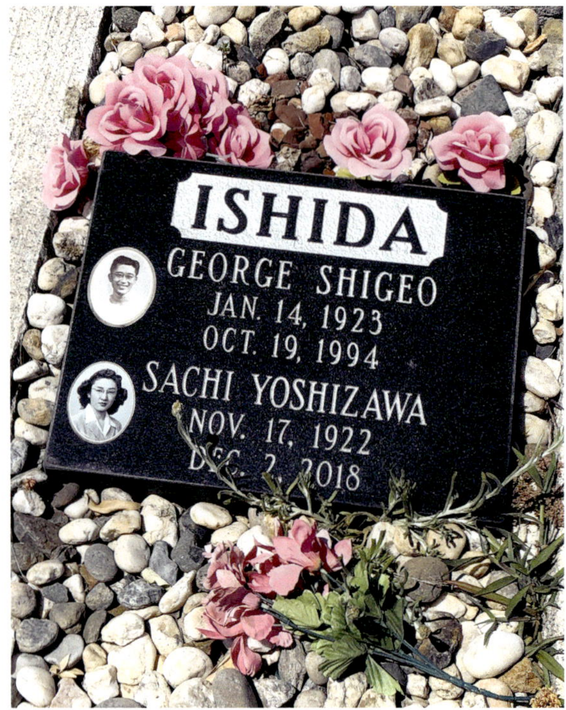

The Ishida family at the Japanese Cemetery in Colma.

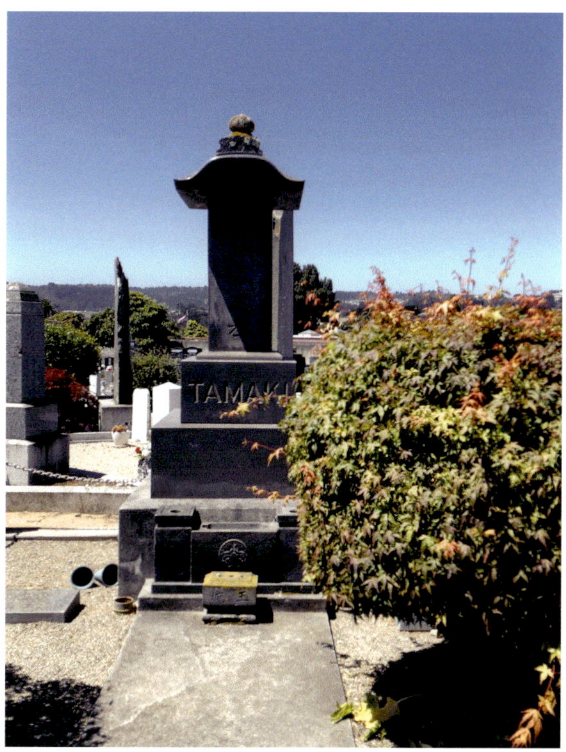

The Tamaki family plot.

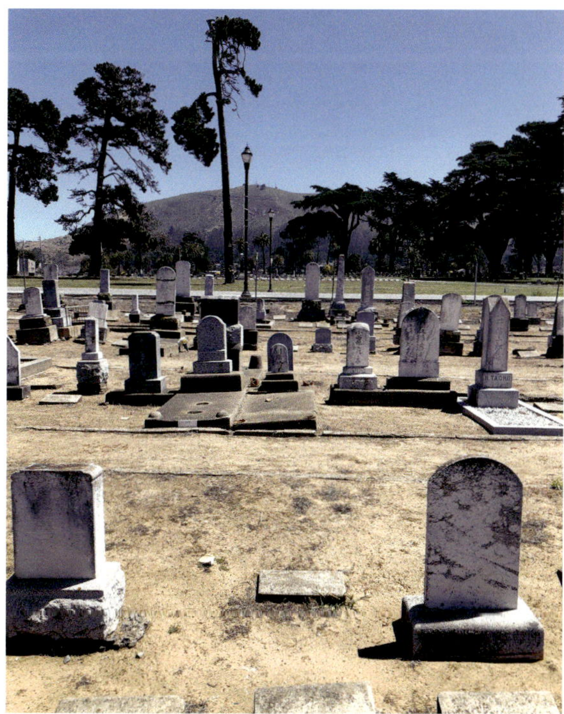

A view of the Victorian-era section (graves moved from San Francisco) at the Japanese Cemetery in Colma.

# 6
# OUT THERE

Just outside the Bay Area there are many cemeteries with pioneers that have rested here since well before California's statehood in 1850. In Bolinas, a small family cemetery expanded into a larger community burial ground behind the local church. Poet and City Lights founder, Lawrence Ferlinghetti, was buried here, next to his mother, in 2021. His headstone is an unassuming granite rock.

In Mendocino, there are two pioneer cemeteries with immigrants born in Norway, Italy, and Germany. The cemetery at the top of the hill boasts a gorgeous view of the historic church and the ocean.

During a visit to Sea Ranch, I was surprised to see a cemetery pop up on my map in Gualala. I had driven through the small town just outside of Sea Ranch and on the way north up the coast many times but never noticed a cemetery. I followed directions down a dirt path and came upon an open gate. Directly to the left, there was a small cemetery there with a few volunteers hard at work, picking weeds. It was pure luck that I had arrived on a Tuesday, the only day the gates are open. The Gualala Cemetery restoration project is not only an attempt to clean up and uncover the cemetery, but it is also a genealogical reclamation of the families and descendants of those buried here.

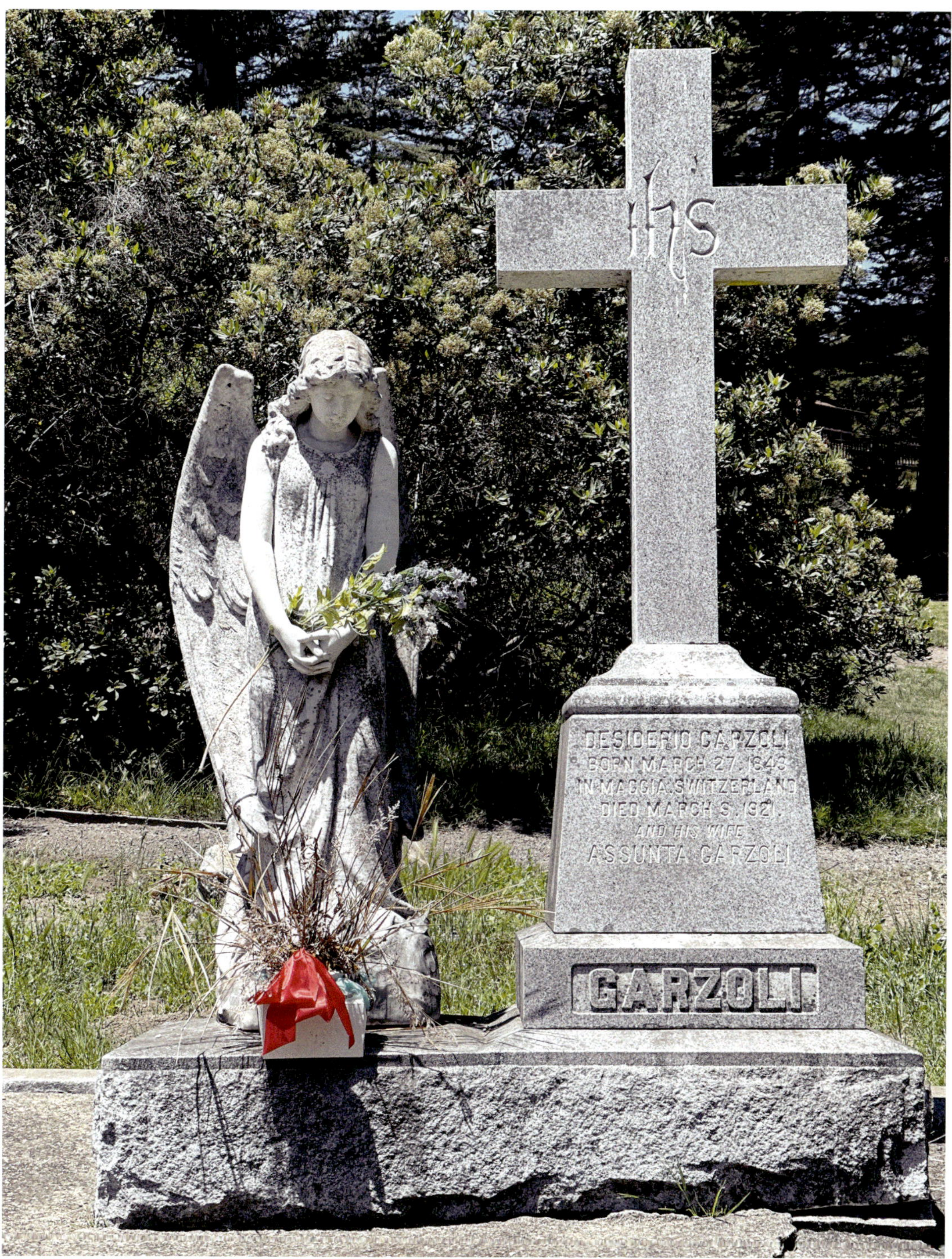



A guardian angel at Bolinas Cemetery.

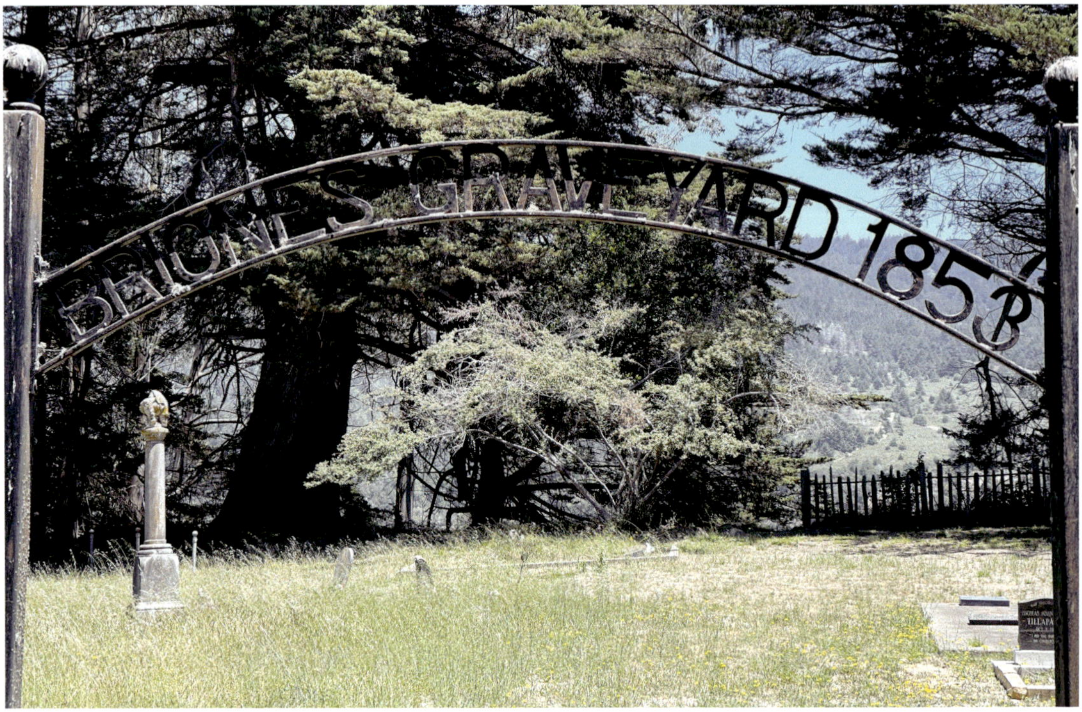

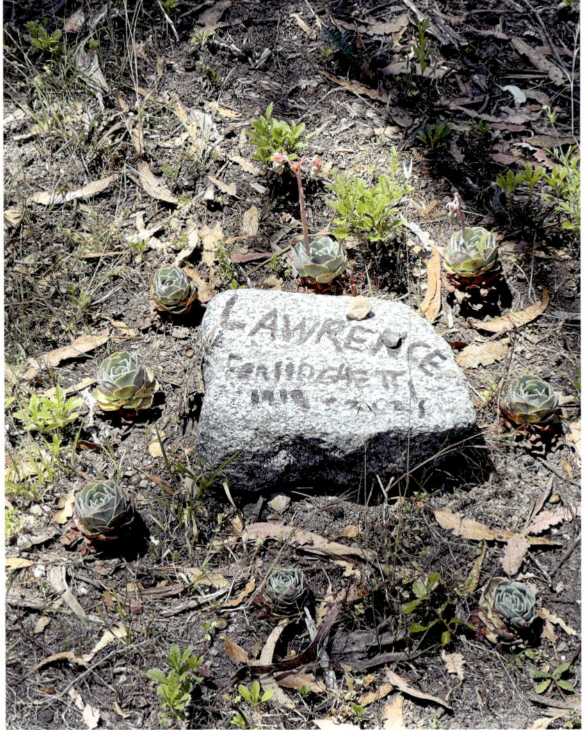

*Above:* Briones Graveyard, a family graveyard established 1853.

*Left:* The resting place of Lawrence Ferlingetti, author and founder of City Lights Books.

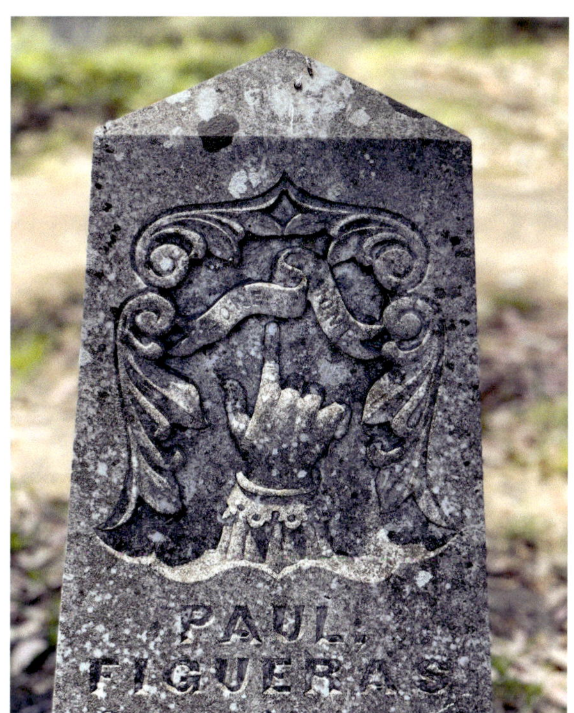

Look up, I'm resting in heaven.

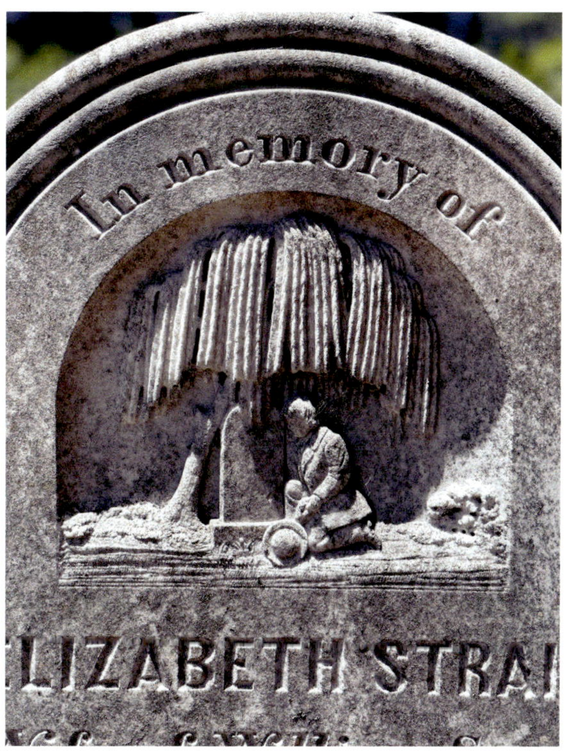

Gorgeous Victorian era
weeping willow memorial.

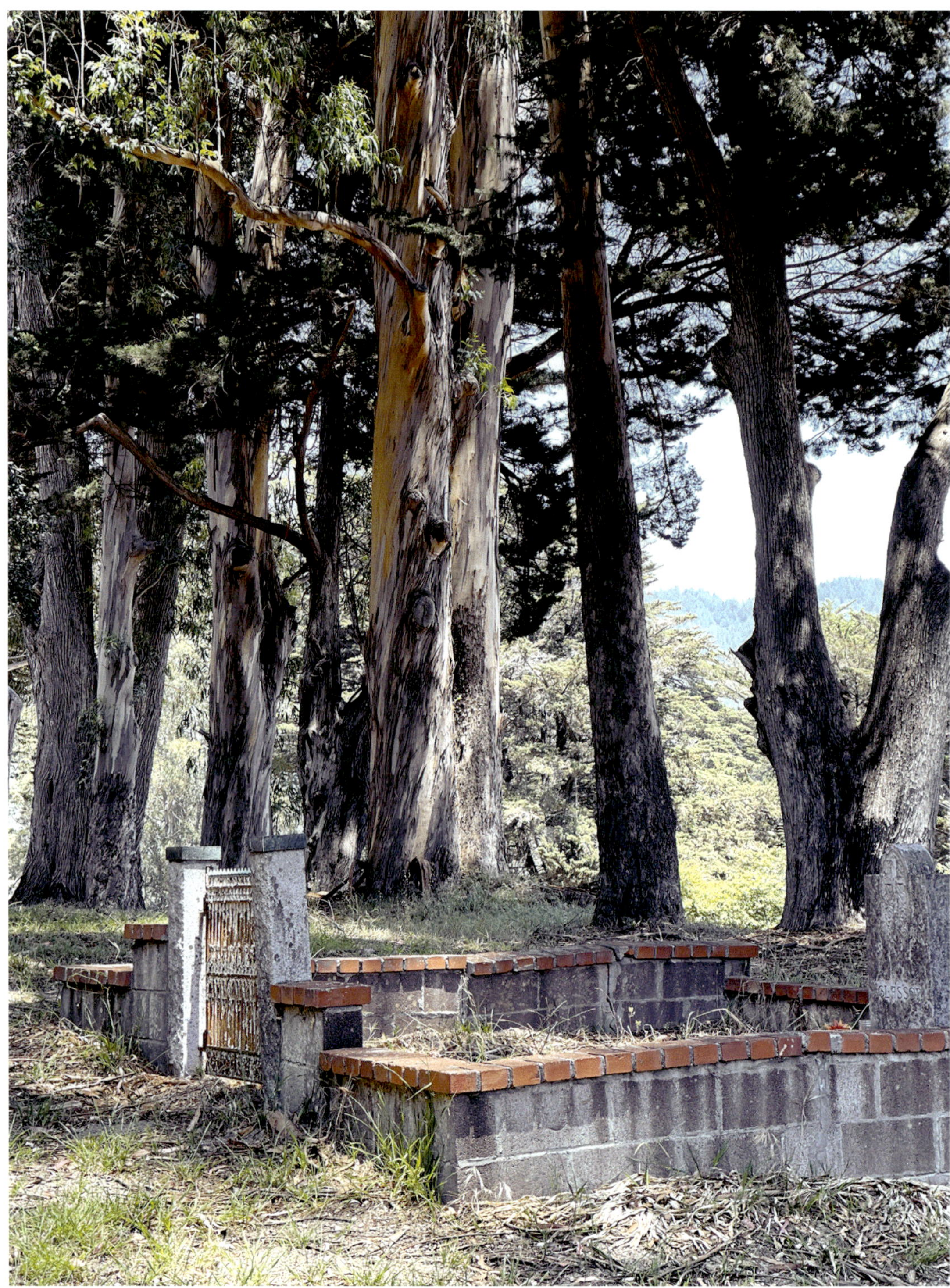

Beautiful redwoods at Bolinas Cemetery.

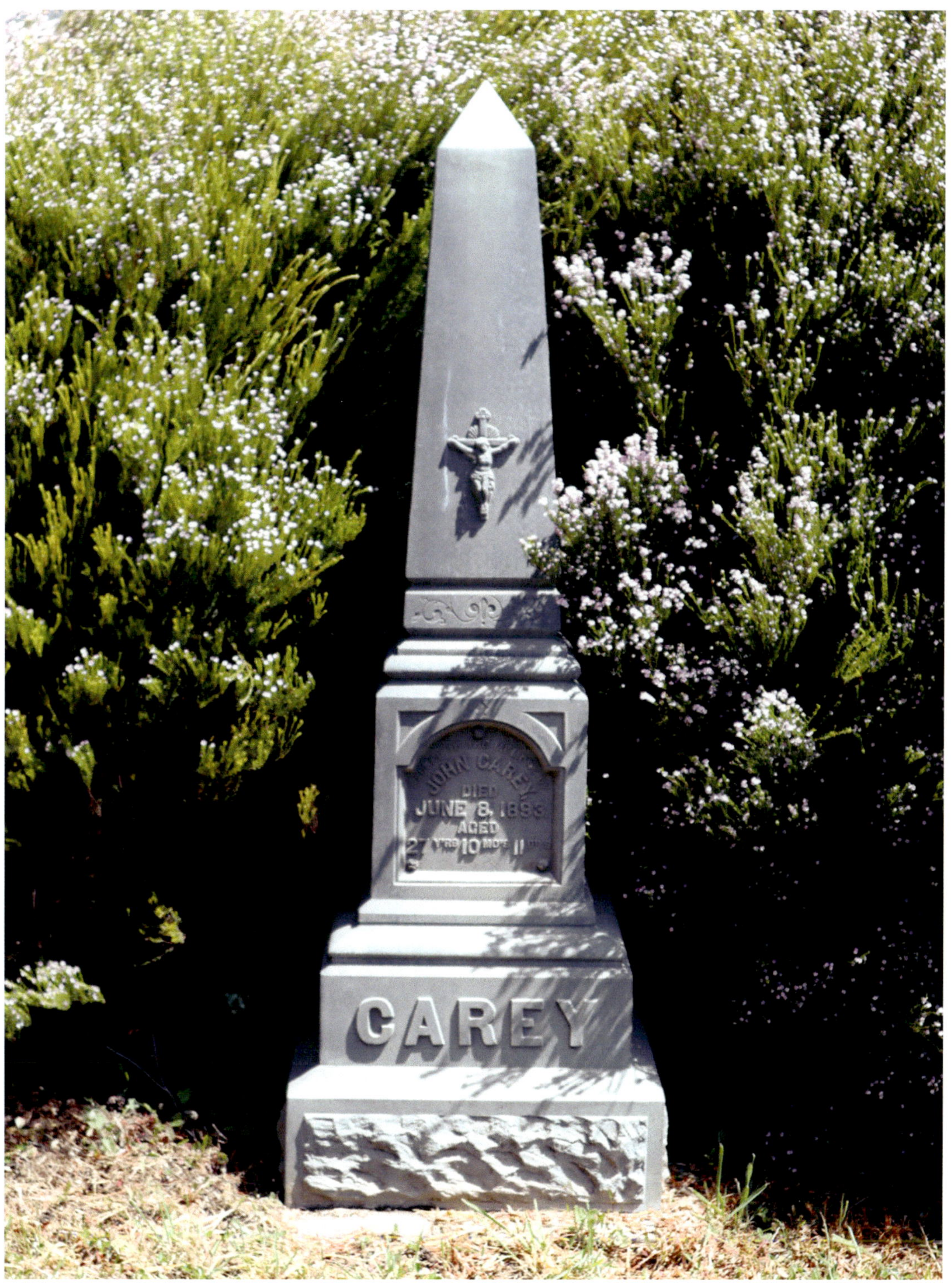



The Carey family plot.

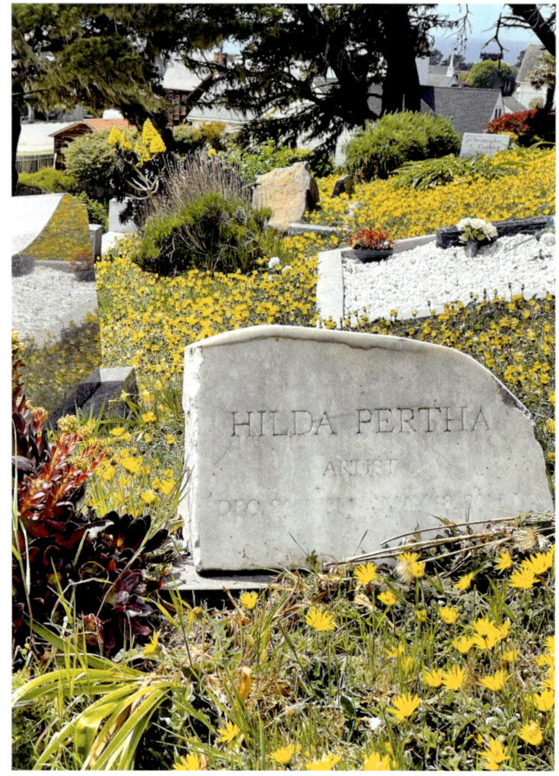

*Left:* Hilda, an artist.

*Below left:* Mother.

*Below right:* A young lady, Maria.

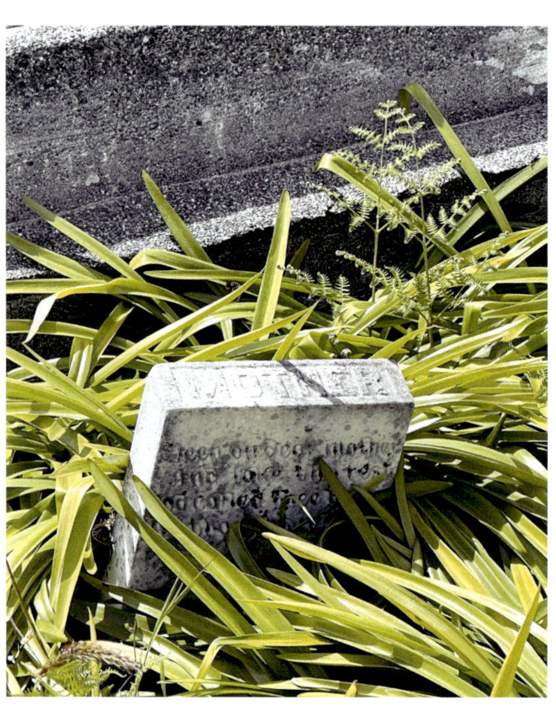

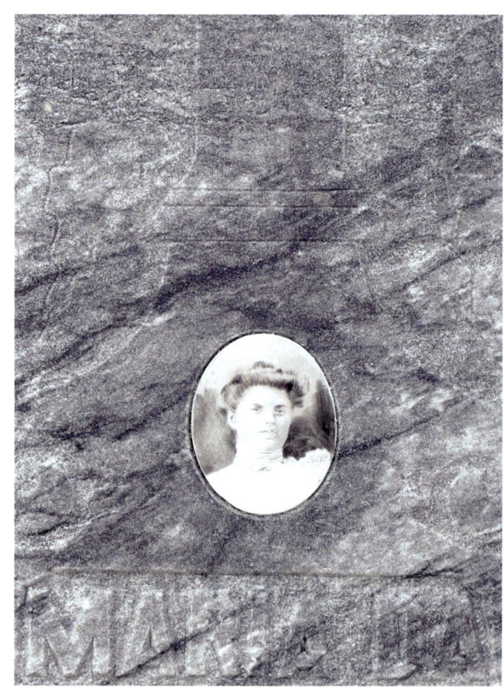

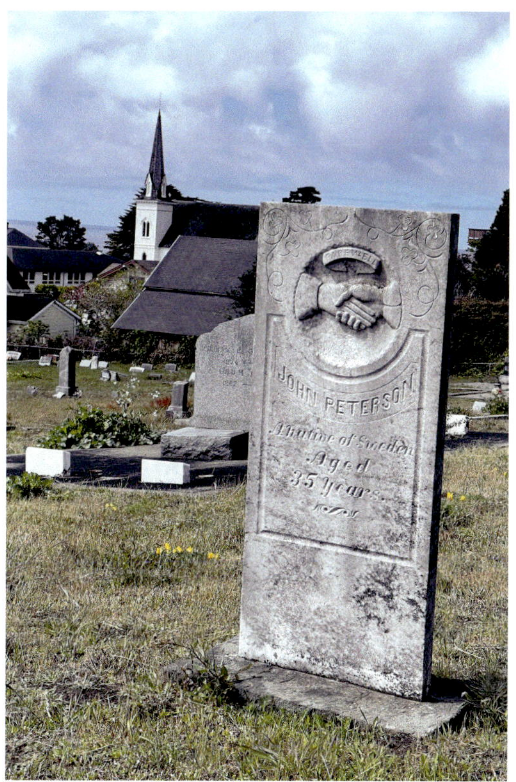

The pioneer cemetery in Mendocino with the church spire in the background.

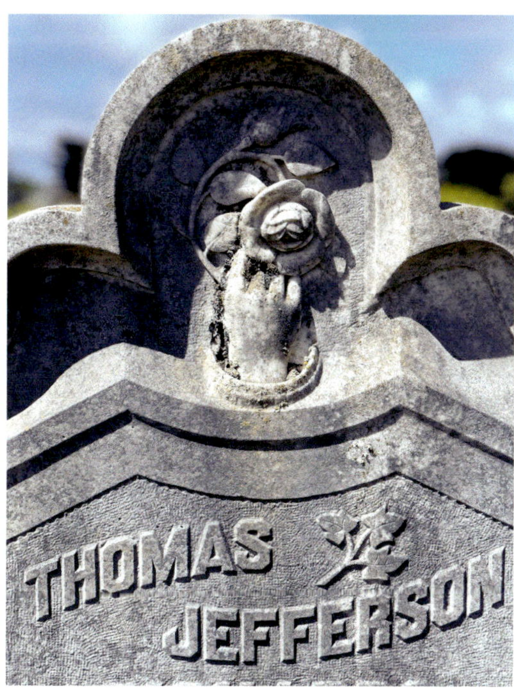


Presidential names were once popular.

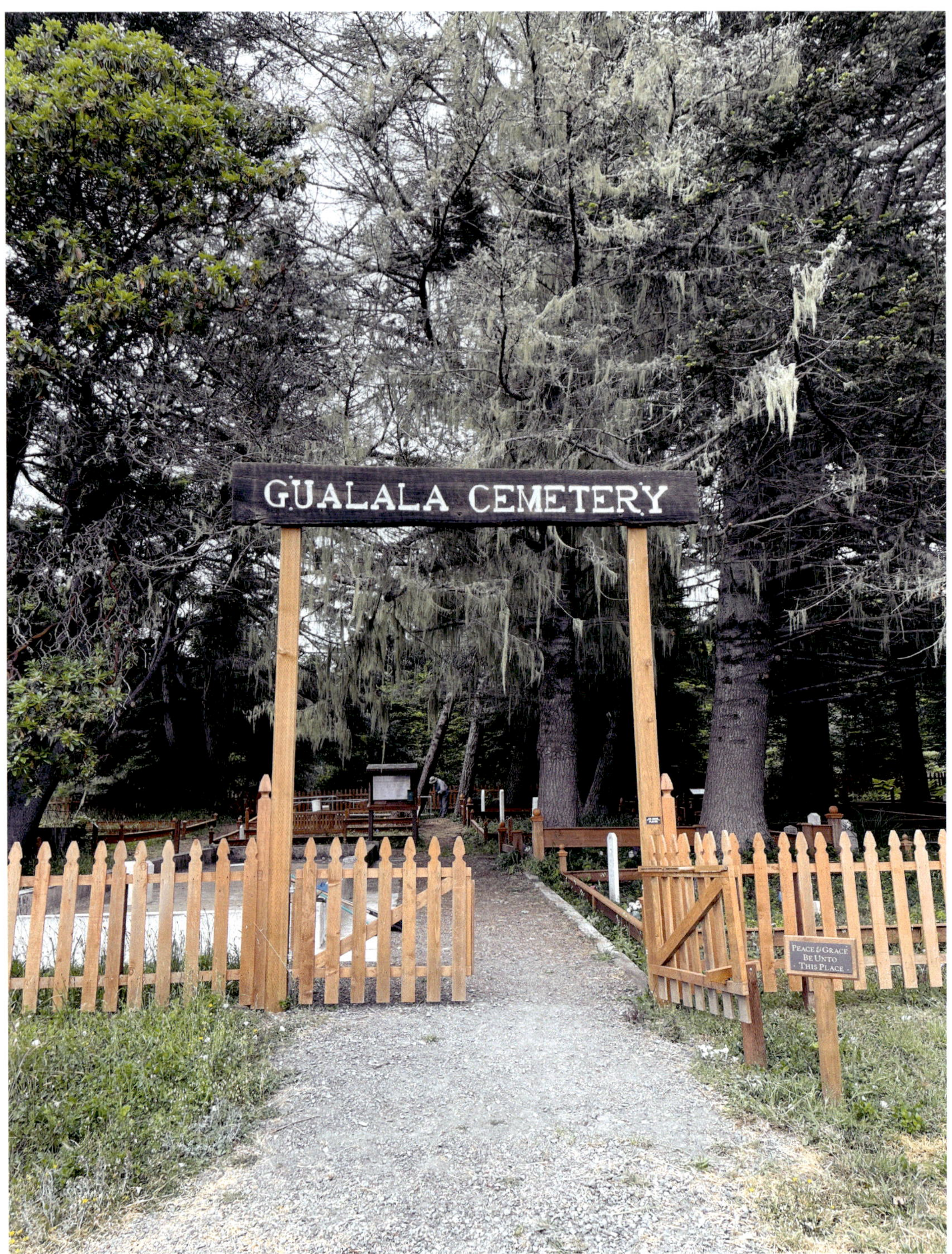


The recently reclaimed and restored Gualala Cemetery.

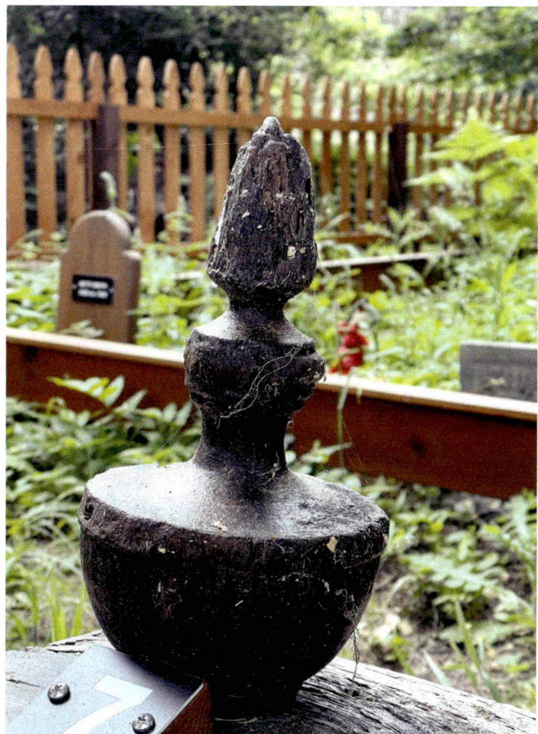

*Right:* Original wooden plot adornments.

*Below left:* The restoration work for this pioneer cemetery is done by volunteers from the community.

*Below right:* A gorgeous, restored marker for Edith with a lily of the valley, symbolizing the death of a young girl.

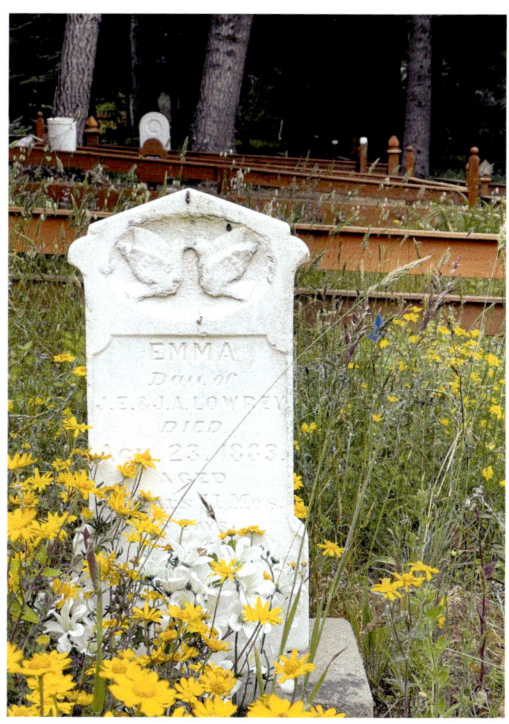

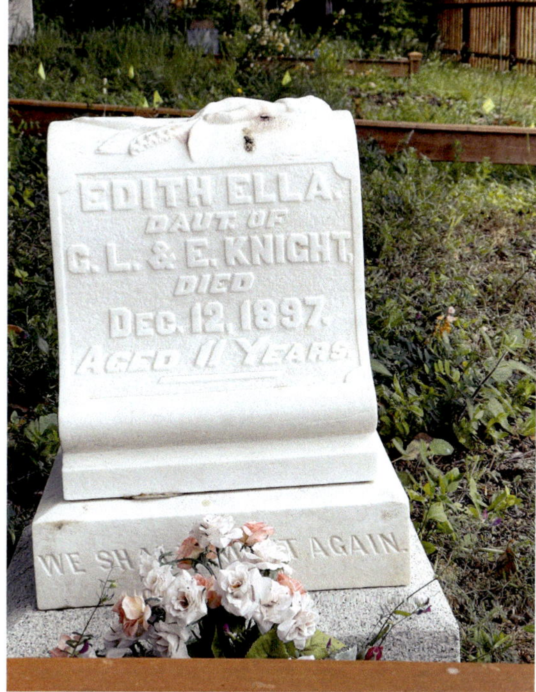

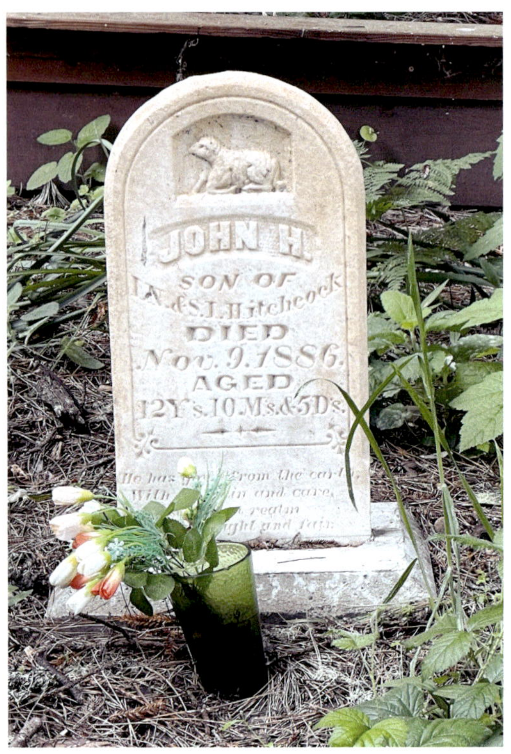

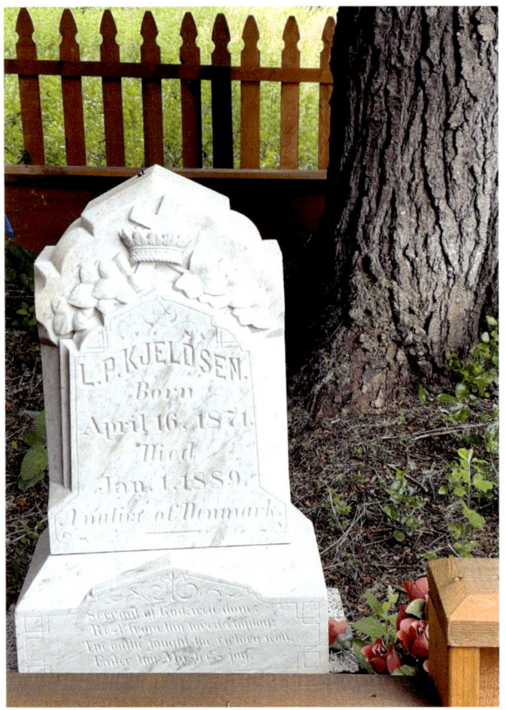

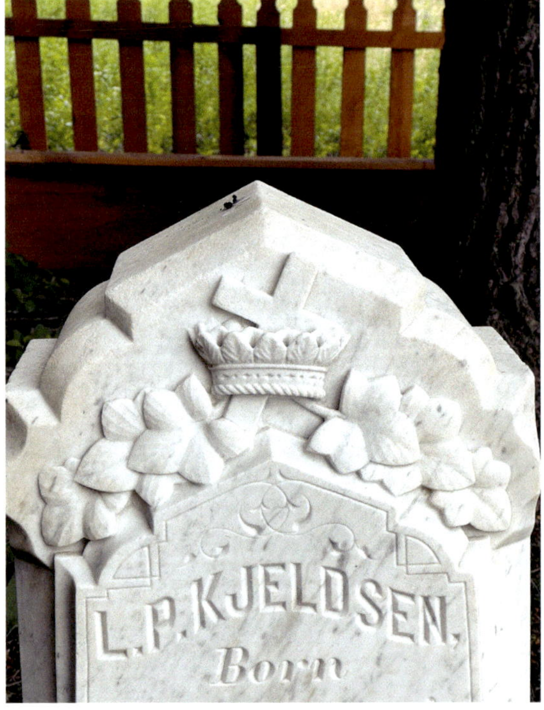

*Left:* Another marker for a child, John, with a lamb symbolizing the loss of a young person.

*Below:* The Kjeldsen tombstone, lovingly restored, wonderfully beautiful.